GRANTA

NEW WORLD

D0103689

29

Editor: Bill Buford
Commissioning Editor: Lucretia Stewart
Assistant Editor: Tim Adams
Managing Editor: Angus MacKinnon
Assistant to the Editor: Ursula Doyle

Publisher/Consultant: Alice Rose George
Financial Manager: Robert Linney
Subscriptions: Gillian Kemp, Carol Harris
Advertising and Circulation: Alison Ormerod

Picture Research: David Brownridge
Design: Chris Hyde
Executive Editor: Pete de Bolla
US Associate Publisher: Anne Kinard, Granta, 250 West 57th Street, Suite 1316, New York, NY 10107.

Editorial and Subscription Correspondence: Granta, 44a Hobson Street, Cambridge CB1 1NL. Telephone: (0223) 315290.
All manuscripts are welcome but must be accompanied by a stamped, self-addressed envelope or they cannot be returned.

Granta is photoset by Cambridge Photosetting Services, Cambridge, England, and printed by Hazell Watson and Viney Ltd, Aylesbury, Bucks.

Granta is published by Granta Publications Ltd and distributed by Penguin Books Ltd, Harmondsworth, Middlesex, England; Viking Penguin Inc., 40 West 23rd St, New York, New York, USA; Penguin Books Australia Ltd, Ringwood, Victoria, Australia; Penguin Books Canada Ltd, 2801 John Street, Markham, Ontario, Canada L3R 1B4; Penguin Books (NZ) Ltd, 182–90 Wairau Road, Auckland 10, New Zealand. This selection copyright © 1989 by Granta Publications Ltd.

Cover by the Senate. Cover photograph by Julian Germain.

Granta 29, Winter 1989

ISBN 014-01-2862-X

SUPPORTED BY THE
EASTERN
Arts

NADINE GORDIMER

THE
WRITING
ESSENTIAL
POLITICS
GESTURE
& PLACES

'The story of an artist's awakening; to literature, to Africa, and to the great ugly reality of Apartheid... the literary value of these essays derives not only from their testamentary power, but also from the range and depth of their preoccupations'
- *Observer*

£5.99

Autumn Highlights from Faber

P.D. JAMES
Devices and Desires
0 571 14178 1 £11.99

ALLAN GURGANUS
Oldest Living Confederate Widow Tells All
0 571 14201 X £12.99

G. CABRERA INFANTE
Three Trapped Tigers
0 571 15369 0 £12.99

GARRISON KEILLOR
We Are Still Married
0 571 14140 4 £11.99

JOAO UBALDO RIBEIRO
An Invincible Memory
0 571 14837 9 £12.99

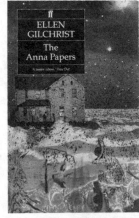

ELLEN GILCHRIST
The Anna Papers
0 571 14097 1 £12.99

CONTENTS

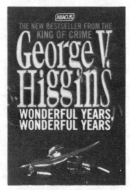
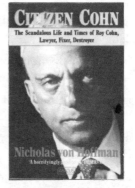

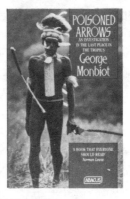

JONATHAN RABAN

NEW WORLD

A t first sight the ship was bigger than the dock in which it floated, a whale sprawled in a hip-bath.

Nine hundred-and-something feet long, 56,000 tons gross, it was a custom-built marine pantechnicon. It had a toppling Hilton hotel mounted at its back end, with a long city block of slotted containers stretching out ahead of it. For the last ten days it had gone tramping round the small seas of Europe, picking up cargo from Le Havre, Antwerp, Rotterdam, Bremen and Gothenburg, and it was now gorged with exports. The car decks, on the water-line and below, were a luxury traffic jam of unplated Jaguars, Porsches and Mercedes. The containers were packed with many thousands of tons of bizarre odds and ends: Swedish matches, French brandy, frozen seal meat, Dutch tulip bulbs, paint, perfume, laughing gas, helium . . . Two containers were bound for Macy's store on Herald Square in Manhattan: one, loaded at Le Havre, was billed on the manifest as 'French wearing apparel'; the other, which had come on at Liverpool, was billed as 'English bric-à-brac'.

The accommodation for the crew of the *Atlantic Conveyor* matched the grandeur of its cargo. I was travelling as a guest of the owners, Cunard Ellerman, and was assigned the cabin of Officer B, high up on the tenth floor of the wedding-cake. Officer B lived well. His cabin was a roomy studio apartment furnished with bookcases, a refrigerator, a king-size bed, a comfortable sofa, a long desk of varnished pine, a cabinet for drinks and glasses, a coffee-table and his own lavatory and shower. Just down the hall, Officer B could swim in the heated pool, put in a sweaty half-hour or so on the squash court, work out in the gym and open his pores in the sauna, before showing up in the Officers Bar and Lounge, where the bonded Scotch was ten pence a measure, and where a new film was shown on the video at eight-fifteen each night.

I spread myself in Officer B's fine quarters and loaded his bookshelves with the accounts of the nineteenth-century visitors and emigrants whose company I meant to keep during the voyage. I'd brought Irving Howe's *World of Our Fathers* and Moses Rischin's *The Promised City*, for their descriptions of Jewish peasants in steerage; Henry Roth's *Call It Sleep*, for the arrival in New York Harbor; Robert Louis Stevenson's *The Amateur Emigrant*; Charles Dickens's *American Notes for General*

11

Circulation. Officer B's cabin compared extravagantly well with the stuffy dormitory-cum-canteen in which Stevenson made his crossing, or Dickens's 'state-room' on the steam-packet, *Britannia*, which turned out to be an 'utterly impracticable, thoroughly hopeless and profoundly preposterous box'. In Officer B's swivel chair, looking out through Officer B's picture window, wondering whether to pick up Officer B's telephone and ask the purser if he could bring me a bottle of Famous Grouse, I felt a tide of resentful envy coming my way from the voyagers on the bookshelf. Ian Jamieson, the purser, said that he'd be around with the whisky in five minutes. I got Stevenson down from the shelf.

> The second cabin is a modified oasis in the very heart of the steerages. Through the thin partition you can hear the steerage passengers being sick, the rattle of tin dishes as they sit at meals, the varied accents in which they converse, the crying of their children terrified by this new experience, or the clean flat smack of the parental hand in chastisement.

The purser showed with the Famous Grouse, together with an electric kettle, a jar of coffee, a carton of milk and a pair of rather pretty cups and saucers. Sailing, he said, had been delayed till tomorrow noon. There would be drinks in the Officers Bar at half-past five, followed by dinner, then a film on the video . . . The emigrants booed and whistled from behind their covers.

When the ship at last began to move, it did so with ponderous delicacy. I was on the bridge, a hundred feet above sea-level and ceremoniously remote from the operations that were going on down in the bows and the stern and on the dock. The silence was churchy. A hushed voice over the radio announced that the stern line was off; another came in to say that the bow was now clear. We were so many storeys up that the only way to tell that the main engine was running was to put our palms on the bridge-console and feel the metal surface tremble, with an even beat, like the skin of a breathing creature. The Sunday-suited pilot stood by the captain's elbow as the enormous ship eased itself, inch by steady inch, away from the wharf. To reach the open estuary, it had to move forward, turn on its axis in a space shorter than its own length, then feed itself into a long double lock that was half as wide as the ship's beam. It was a camel-through-the-eye-of-a-needle job, and I stood holding a rail, waiting for the million-pound crunch.

No one raised his voice. Wives and children were inquired after, the weather was grumbled over, Liverpool's home draw at Anfield on Saturday was derided, while the *Atlantic Conveyor* squeezed itself in, spun itself round and shrank itself into the lock.

'How much clearance do we have on either side?'

'Oh—a good eighteen inches.'

While the lock filled to bring the ship level with the open water outside, we enjoyed a view of a ragged alp of rusty junk. The First Officer said, 'Liverpool's chief export. Scrap.'

'Who's the lucky recipient?'

'The Japs. It all comes back to Liverpool eventually . . . as Toyotas and Hondas.'

We slid gingerly forward, feeling with our bows for the cross-tide at the entrance, made a slow turn to starboard and began threading our way north through the sand- and mud-banks of the Crosby Channel.

I'd never been on a ship as big as the *Conveyor* and found it hard to adjust to its silence, its absence of palpable motion. It was as if we were at anchor while the Mersey estuary and Liverpool Bay were being slowly dragged away from under our hull. I was used to seeing the sea at close quarters, to treating each wave with respectful deference, but from the patrician height of the *Conveyor*'s bridge I saw the Irish Sea (which I knew as an easily roused bully) humbly licking our boots.

The *Conveyor* lorded it over the small fry of struggling trawlers and tinpot freighters. We were the biggest ship in the sea, we were America-bound. There was a splendid arrogance about the way we drove our cargo of coloured containers far ahead of us into the murk while the mountains of Snowdonia, dramatically and perversely sunlit, closed with us, fine on our port bow.

With a very faint churring sound, somewhere deep down in her lower intestinal arrangements, the ship moved to Full Ahead. 17.5 knots.

Captain Jackson came over to where I was standing. 'Well, what do you think of the ship so far?' He was a squarely built, deliberative Welshman, who counted out his words like coins and whose voice had a dry, North Walian creak to it.

I said: 'It feels like going to sea in a block of flats. It's so motionless. Does she never roll?'

'Oh, yes. She rolls.'

He checked the glowing bronze screen of one of the radar sets on the bridge, targeted a white blip on the six-mile ring, glanced up at the digital read-out of our speed, and studied the anemometer, which showed forty-five knots of apparent wind on our port bow. The *Conveyor* was moving at full speed, perfectly upright, through a near gale.

'It takes a lot to make her move, but when she moves, she moves.'

In the winter of 1986, Captain Jackson said, the *Conveyor* ran into a violent storm 300 miles east of Newfoundland. The tops of the waves were higher than the level of the bridge. The needle of the anemometer was glued solid to eighty-five knots, its highest reading. The actual speed of the west wind was 100 knots, perhaps more.

'She was making forty-degree rolls?'

'You mean rolling twenty degrees each way?'

'No. Forty degrees to port. Forty degrees to starboard.'

I couldn't see it. In my view, if you cant a floating block of flats over at forty degrees, it falls into the sea with an enormous splash and doesn't come up again. Somehow the *Conveyor* had managed to retain her footing and return to the vertical, despite the towering, top-heavy weight of her superstructure.

For two days the crew had fought to keep her facing up into the wind and sea. As she hit each new wave, her bows had 'fallen off', and the ship had done her best to slew sideways. The screw kept on coming out of the water and at one stage the engine failed. For a time, while the engineers worked to get the main engine back on line (with errant tractors threatening to fall in on their heads), Captain Jackson had kept the ship's head up to the wind with the bow-thrusters—ancillary propellers in the front of the ship, normally used only for manoeuvring in harbour.

'And if she had been caught broadside?'

'God only knows what would have happened.' He checked his instruments again, and made a slow, dry, Welsh inventory of that voyage. 'We had a lot of cargo damage. One man was injured. He still has the scar. The accommodation was in a terrible state. After thirty hours up here, I went down to my cabin; it was *unrecognizable*.'

Leaning forward, hands planted on the console, his meaty fingers spread wide, he was reading the sea. He searched the horizon from end to end, and nodded. 'Yes. She rolls. When we get round the corner of Ireland and meet the swell . . . she'll roll a bit then.'

In the ballroom-sized Officer's Dining-Room, the diners had all known each other for so long, and had sat down to eat with each other so often, that conversation had been reduced to a sort of gruff Morse. If you were in on the code, a single word could do the job of an entire story.

'Meatloaf,' said Donald, one of the second officers.

The second engineer, the electrical officer and Donald's colleague, Vince, chuckled clubbishly, as at the end of some elaborate tale of malarkey, while the radio officer touched his mouth with his napkin and went self-deprecatingly pink. It was a tough world for a stranger to horn in on.

After dinner, we withdrew formally to the bar for coffee and 'stickies'. Stickies were liqueurs—tots of Tia Maria, Cointreau and Drambuie—and these ladylike, sugary concoctions signalled an abrupt change in the tenor of the talk. We were in the drawing-room now and could gossip cosily about life ashore; about wives, children, girl-friends, mortgages, cars, house improvements. Helen, the Chief's wife, and Wee Helen, his daughter, a schoolgirl of sixteen, were now the focal centre of our circle—the official representatives of the families we'd left at home. We talked curtains, in-laws, CSE exams and summer holidays, while the sea began to heap outside the window and the wind made lonely fluting sounds down the ship's empty corridors. Peering through the glass, I saw lights on the Irish coast and recognized them as old acquaintances. There was Wicklow, to the north-west, making its

15

triple wink every fifteen seconds—and, up ahead of us, the Arklow Lanby buoy, flashing twice every twelve seconds. Before, I'd always fought anxiously to identify them as they disappeared behind the tops of waves, and had been worried sick about getting too close to the line of offshore sandbanks that they marked. Up here, nursing a sticky and chatting to Wee Helen about her set passages in *Hamlet*, I saw them as pretty twinkles in the night.

I climbed up to the darkened bridge, from where the sea was looking more like a real sea now. The wind had started to cry in the rigging and in the tall stalks of the radar antennae. The anemometer showed fifty-five knots, dead on the nose—or about forty knots of true wind, a full gale.

I made myself a mug of coffee in the chart-room at the back of the bridge. A fax machine was stuttering out a silver weather-map of the Atlantic. On another day, in another vessel, this brittle, smudgy document would have reduced me to panic and a desperate run for a safe harbour.

Captain Jackson came in, scanned the map, and said, 'Yes, looks as if we might be in for a bit of a blow in a day or two . . . This hurricane here—' he pointed somewhere down in the region of Bermuda, 'Helene . . . seems to be changing direction now. See, she was going along this track, westwards; now she's started to head north. We'll be keeping an eye on her over the next few days.' He spoke of this hurricane as indulgently as a teacher might have spoken of a mildly naughty child in their class. I didn't at all like the look of Helene; she was a dense black stain, with her isobars coiled as tightly as the loops of a watch-spring.

'Very probably she'll peter out long before she gets to us. She'll just be another low, like the one we're in.'

I thought, forty degrees to port, forty degrees to starboard, wave tops higher than the bridge, engine failure, caught broadside . . .

At lunch the next day, both Helen and Wee Helen were white-faced and queasy. Wee Helen was staring into her plate of oxtail soup as if she'd just noticed a hatch of mosquito larvae wriggling about in it. The captain was trying to introduce a more cheerful note.

'It looks as if we'll have a lovely day tomorrow—there's a nice ridge of high pressure coming up. We'll have lost this wind by the evening, and after that we should have a flat calm for a day at least. Lots of sunshine. You'll be able to take those folding loungers out on to the afterdeck and put in some sunbathing time . . .'

Water slopped in the jug. A spoon slid across the table under its own steam. Wee Helen headed for her cabin, making swimming motions as she floundered up the slope of the dining-room floor.

'It's not the rolling I mind,' her mother said. 'It's this pitching I can't stand. Anyway, like I always say on every voyage, this is *definitely* the last time.'

'Is that a threat or a promise?' said her husband, tucking, with unkind gusto, into his plate of bangers and mash.

'What about the other Helen?' I asked the captain.

'Oh—Helene, you mean? They demoted her this morning. They've got her down to a tropical storm now. I don't think she's going to be any serious problem.' But there was a note in his voice which suggested that he might be putting a comforting gloss on the facts for Mrs Meek's benefit. After lunch I sneaked a look at the latest print-out from the fax machine.

TROPICAL STORM 'HELENE' 37.5N 47.0W EXPECTED 47.5N 37W BY 30/0600 GMT. THEN BECOMING EXTRA-TROPICAL BUT REMAINING A VERY INTENSE STORM, EXPECTED 58N 26W, 950 BY 0100 GMT, 63N, 19W UNCHANGED BY 0200 GMT, 67N 07W 960 BY 03/000 GMT. BRACKNELL W'FAX.

At 950 millibars, the atmospheric pressure of Helene's heart was very low indeed—a hungry vacuum trying to fill itself by sucking in the surrounding air and making it spin, counter-clockwise, like a plug-hole draining water from a bath. This whirling mass of unstable air, with winds of seventy-five to ninety knots at its centre, was moving north-east up the Atlantic at about twenty-five miles an hour. The *Conveyor*, on her Great Circle course to Nova Scotia, was heading on what looked to me like a probable collision-course with angry Helene, whose temper, according to the forecast, was declining from hysterical to just plain furious. Before hurricanes achieved sexual equality (Helene had been preceded, a fortnight before, by Gilbert, who had wrecked the West Indies and torn a broad swathe through northern Mexico), they used to be called

17

'whirlygirls'. The more closely I looked at the chart, spreading the points of a pair of dividers between where we were and where Helene was going, the more suspicious I became that we had a firm date with a whirlygirl.

Out in front, the containers stretched ahead in railway-line perspective, almost to vanishing-point. The rectangles of ochre, green, rust-red, grey and blue looked like someone's inept copy of a Mondrian as they dug their way through the breaking swell. I needed a pair of binoculars to see what was happening to the front of the ship. I got the stubby foremast in focus and watched it twisting stiffly from side to side as the whole structure of the *Conveyor* groaned and flexed, trying to fit itself to the uncomfortable sea.

The wind was blowing from west-north-west at Gale Force 8 and gusting to Severe Gale 9. Vince, the officer of the watch, put the swell at thirty feet, though from the bridge it looked less.

'That's the danger of a ship this size. Up here, you're so far removed from the elements, you get blasé. If you were down on Three Deck now, that sea would look bloody terrifying. High as houses. And in this sort of weather you have to know exactly what you're asking the ship to do. Otherwise you'll overstretch her.'

I didn't care for the sound of 'overstretch'. Studied through binoculars, the torque looked painful. There was a distinct bow in the line of containers, while the bridge and the foremast were rolling in opposite directions.

'That's good. It shows she's got some give in her.'

Down in the cabin, it was hard to concentrate on reading. Dickens was drowned out by the drum-roll noise of the swells as they came jolting through the hull. *Rivets*, I thought, and instantly heard them popping like buttons all over the ship. *Metal fatigue*, I thought, and lost myself in a maze of empty-headed speculations about molecules growing fatally sleepy under stress. At dinner, I felt aggrieved when someone, at last acknowledging that we were eventually going to meet up with Helene, or at least tangle with her skirts, talked of 'this blow that's coming up'. To live in a world where Force-8-gusting-9 didn't even count as 'a blow' struck me as dangerously unnatural.

After the ritual dispensation of stickies, a group of officers sat down around the table in the bar to play *Colditz*, shaking dice and drawing cards to break their way out of a prison camp; *as well they might*, I thought. Wee Helen was sufficiently recovered to join them. I looked in two hours later and they were still at it, with Wee Helen trapped, in fiction as in fact, in the Officers Quarters, while Dave, the radio officer, was making a break for the Perimeter Wire, as the ship slammed and shuddered her way through the dark.

We were shrinking. We seemed to be a lot shorter and a lot closer to the water than before. With nothing to measure itself against now except the open Atlantic, the ship, so enormous in Liverpool, so lordly in the Irish Sea, was dwindling into a dot, a cell of dry little British jokes, fine little British caste distinctions and surprisingly formal British manners. I had once spent three weeks aboard a coaster whose crew had behaved like a rollicking gang as they nipped and tucked between the ports of Cornwall, France, the Netherlands, Northumberland and Lincolnshire. On the *Conveyor*, things were very different, and it was as if the bigness of the sea itself had subdued us, made us more polite and respectful of the terms of the social code that goes with sailing under a Red Ensign. We talked in lowered voices. We spent hours just staring at water, watching it change colour as it bulged and contracted, bulged and contracted, or went sifting lazily past the side of the hull. We didn't seem to be going any*where*; we were merely *going*, intransitively, like the movement of a clock.

'At times like this,' said the officer of the watch, 'the captain's job is to be like a fire-extinguisher in a box, with a sign on the front saying, "Break Glass Only In Emergency."'

We had reached the stage where not only was it impossible properly to imagine the land we were headed for, it was impossible properly to remember the land we had left. There was simply too much sea around to think of anything else but sea. It sopped up every other thought in one's head. It must have been at this stage that the emigrants began to shed their *emi* prefix, and turned into pure migrants, as oblivious as birds to anything except the engrossing mechanics of their passage.

'Anything happening?' asked Vince, relieving Donald of his watch.

'Nothing. Nothing at all.'

'The pressure's starting to drop,' Vince said; and it was—the barograph needle was sliding from 1026 down to 1025.

'When will we meet Helene, do you think?'

'Not for hours yet. Not till well into tomorrow morning, and then she should be a good 300 miles or so off.'

I was surprised to see so many birds so far from land, and armed with the captain's bird book I set to naming them. The little black-and-white ones that skated and pattered in our wake were stormy petrels; the bulky brown high-fliers were skuas; the gull-like birds, riding the wind at cabin-level and matching themselves inch for inch against the speed of the ship, were fulmars. But the really fanciable birds, the aeronautical aces, were the Manx shearwaters. They hugged the waves on wings as stiff as those of model aeroplanes, gliding, banking, swivelling, diving, as they followed the continuously changing contour of the water at a distance so close that you couldn't tell where the face of the wave ended and the wing-tip of the bird began. They seemed to be courting death by drowning, and as the waves grew steeper and whiter, the exploits of the shearwaters grew more audaciously cavalier. I was thrilled by these birds; it was as though they had been constructed out of balsa-wood, tissue-paper and dope: they made the sullen North Atlantic look fun.

There was now a bilious tinge to the rim of sky ahead of us; a streaky, greeny-yallery look, as if Helene had been lightly currying it in turmeric, saffron and coriander.

'That's a classic storm sunset,' Donald said, as if it was exactly what he'd been hoping for. The *Conveyor* stood on course.

Hurricanes, or tropical cyclones, are hatched in the Cape Verde Basin, ten degrees or more north of the Equator, off the coasts of Senegal, Guinea, Sierra Leone. They feed on moisture from the sea, charging themselves with water that has been warmed over the tropical summer. As this water vapour condenses in the air it releases energy in the form of heat, and the infant hurricane begins to spin. Moving like a top across the surface of the Atlantic, it crosses the Fifteen Twenty Fracture Zone and the Barracuda Ridge, gaining speed and confidence as it goes. By the time it hits the Puerto Rican Trench, it is a mature storm with a name of its own (given to it by NOAA, the happy acronym of the National Oceanic and Atmospheric Administration of the United States). Here, it either keeps on going west into the Caribbean or, like Helene, swerves north and east up the middle of the ocean, where the coldness of the sea usually reduces it to a tame Atlantic Depression.

Helene had more stamina than most of her kind. She was now past the fortieth parallel, but the weather-fax machine was still reporting winds of seventy-five knots at her centre (a hurricane-force wind starts at sixty-four knots). We were more than 300 miles away from her now, but inching closer, our speed reduced by half. The *Conveyor's* anemometer was showing fifty to fifty-five knots of true wind, as the ship bullied her tonnage through the sea.

Trying to sleep, I was unpleasantly teased by the image of the *Conveyor* as a giant Italian bread-stick. She was so long, so slender, so brittle—why couldn't the waves simply snap her between their fingers? Then she turned into a shunting train. For some reason best known to himself, the driver was ramming the buffers, again and again and again. Then she became my own boat, a cork on a billow, and the slow recollection of her actual tonnage, her huge and ponderous stability at sea, worked on me like a shot of Valium. I woke only when I found myself sliding, half in, half out of the bed.

It was still dark. The ship was leaning over to starboard, pinned there by the steady brunt of the wind. A cautious uphill walk to Officer B's picture window turned out to be an unrewarding exercise. It was impossible to see out for the gluey rime of wet salt on the pane.

Up on the bridge, I found that someone had broken the captain out of his glass box, for he was standing by the wheel in slippers, pyjamas and dressing-gown.

'Morning,' he treated me to a polite nod. 'Bit of a windy morning we've got today.' Slow-smiling, slow-moving, comfortably wrapped in paisley, Captain Jackson had the knack of conjuring around himself a broad ambit of suburban calm and snugness. Far from piloting his ship through the remains of a hurricane on the North Atlantic, he might have been pottering among the geraniums in his greenhouse on the morning of the local flower-show.

'Didn't you sleep well?'

'Fine,' I said, doing my best to match his tone. 'I just wanted to

21

see what was going on up here.'

'There's nothing much to see. We're down to five knots at present. The wind's come up to about sixty.'

The howl somewhere behind and below us was the ship's screw, taking a brief airing out of the water.

I tried to interest the captain in the drama of the storm. I told him of Dickens's passage in January 1842, when the *Britannia* steam-ship had met weather so bad that Thackeray had suspected Dickens of making it up for literary effect. On his own Atlantic crossing, Thackeray had put his doubts to the captain of his ship and been told that the *Britannia* had indeed been lucky to have survived one of the most famously awful storms on record. I quoted Dickens's magnificent description of being tumbled about in a small ship on a wild sea:

> The water-jug is plunging and leaping like a lively dolphin; all the smaller articles are afloat, except my shoes, which are stranded on a carpet-bag, high and dry, like a couple of coal-barges. Suddenly I see them spring into the air, and behold the looking-glass, which is nailed to the wall, sticking fast upon the ceiling. At the same time the door entirely disappears, and a new one is opened in the floor. Then I begin to comprehend that the state-room is standing on its head.
>
> Before it is possible to make any arrangements at all compatible with this novel state of things, the ship rights. Before one can say 'Thank Heaven!' she wrongs again.

'Yes,' Captain Jackson said. 'Its good. It's . . . vivid. But when he says *wrongs*, that's not a nautical term he's using there. *Righting herself*, yes; *wronging herself*—no, I don't think you'll find that term has ever been used at sea. It gives away the fact that he wasn't really a seaman, doesn't it?'

With this unanswerable piece of scholarship, the captain went back to glooming over the wheel.

In the chart-room, the barograph was bottoming-out at 994. Helene's centre, about 250 miles off, was supposed to be 950, so we were on the rim of a deep cone of pressure. Five miles to a millibar is a very steep gradient in a weather system. On the faxed map of the Atlantic, it looked as if we'd sailed into a black hole in the ocean, with the isobars packed so tightly together that you couldn't see the gaps between them. I scanned the deck log, to see if the captain was holding out on me, but the only entry in the 'Comments' column was *Pitching easily*, which seemed a characteristically Jacksonian description of our thundering ride over this warm, alpine sea.

All day, and for most of the next night, the wind stayed up at storm-force, but it was veering. It slowly hauled itself round from south to south-west and then to west, as Helene went north ahead of us, and these shifts confused the sea. The waves began to pile up on top of each other's shoulders. They crashed into each other and exploded into pyramids of froth. By noon, the ship was forced to heave-to. With her engine slowed and her bows pointed up to the weather, she lay in the sea like an enormous log, making no progress over the ground at all.

There were few takers for lunch. The ship's kitchen sounded like a poorly conducted steel band. An incoming tide of gravy washed over the edge of the plate and made a black pool on the table-cloth. I asked the chief engineer how his wife and daughter were.

'They've both got their sheets pulled over their heads and they've turned their faces to the wall.'

In the tropical aquarium, the fish were having a bad time. Most of their habitat had been uprooted from its floor of coloured gravel and now floated on the surface of the water, which was slopping about and spilling over on to the floor. The big striped angel-fish was beating on the glass with its fins, its mouth framing round O's of panic as it tried to recover its lost equilibrium.

Lying hove-to is a state of mind. You mark time in a world that tilts and slides a lot but is going nowhere. You can't remember when it wasn't like this and you can see no particular reason why there should ever be an end to it. The tangled, shaggy ocean strikes you as the ultimate emblem of meaningless activity. For as far as you can see, it goes on heaping itself up and pulling itself to bits. There is something profoundly numbing in the monotonous grandeur of the thing. Staring at it makes you feel as empty-headed as the angel-fish.

T he next day, the wind was down to a Force 7 out of the north-west—an easy breeze, by the *Conveyor*'s disdainful standards—and the two Helens were back on station.

'But when do we see *life*, Captain?'

'Not long to go now, Mrs Meek. Not long now.'

Everyone was impatient for land. We had picked up the scent of North America and it was suddenly real enough to plan on.

Sometime in the small hours, we had crossed on to the Grand Banks, an enormous apron of sandy flats that fans out south and east from the coasts of Newfoundland and Nova Scotia. Here the cold water of the south-going Labrador Current collides with the warm water of the Gulf Stream as it bends east towards Europe. This sudden mixing of hot and cold produces the chilly steam in which the area is almost continuously enshrouded. It also produces the kind of busy, circulating, aerated water in which krill and zooplankton breed, and the food-chain that starts with krill and zooplankton ends with cod, whales and man.

John Cabot discovered the Grand Banks in 1497, on the return voyage from his search for the North-West Passage to Cathay. Over the Banks, his men (aboard the tiny ship, the *Mathew*) found cod shoaling so densely that they only had to lower baskets over the side to bring them up groaning with fish.

It was a miraculous draught of fishes—an image that fitted wonderfully well with the theological rhetoric in which so much of the European colonization of America was conducted. The New World was Canaan, the land across the water that God promised to the Israelites. It was a moral duty to 'plant a Christian habitation and regiment' there, to 'redeem the people of the Newfound land and those parts from out of the captivity of that spiritual Pharaoh, the devil.' Cabot's baskets of fish, with their powerful echo of the disciples casting their nets on the other side, were seen as happy confirming portents that the conquest of America was an evangelical mission.

The view from the *Conveyor*'s bridge was of a watery world so dank and sun-starved that it was hard to imagine anyone being thrilled by it. Yet in the sixteenth century the fish of the Grand Banks inspired as much excitement as the gold, spices and tobacco of the southern discoveries. In Hakluyt's *Voyages* the Banks earn as much space as Florida and the West Indies. They were the place where fishermen's tall stories came true. By 1578—nearly thirty years before the settlement of Virginia and more than forty before the arrival of the colonists in Massachusetts—an adventurer called Anthony Parkhurst wrote a letter to Hakluyt in which he reported that he had counted about 380 fishing vessels working the Banks during the previous summer. There had been fifty English boats; the rest were Spanish, French and Portuguese. In 1583, Edward Hayes, a ship's captain on the Gilbert expedition, called the Grand Banks 'the most famous fishing in the world'.

It is a hard fact to grasp. Europe was not fished-out. There were huge stocks of cod in the North Sea and the eastern Atlantic. Although the Church (in England, the Crown) had stimulated the fishing industry by turning Friday into a pan-European fish-eating day, the demand can't have been so great as to force a crossing of the Atlantic in order to meet it. Yet the fishermen came.

They were the first Europeans to make themselves at home in America. They fished the Grand Banks from April to July every year, traded with the Indians, laid up stocks of gear and provisions in the natural harbours of Newfoundland, Cape Breton Island and Nova Scotia.

The Russians, working along the extreme easterly fringe of the Banks, were the last survivors of the international floating city of boats which used to fish over Whale Bank, Green Bank, St Pierre Bank, Misaine, Banquereau, Canso and the rest. Everyone on the *Conveyor* could remember the time when these few hundred miles were an intricate slalom course, as the ship twisted and dodged through the fishing fleet, more often than not in thick fog. When Canada increased its fishing limit to 200 miles in the 1970s, the Grand Banks emptied of boats. An hour after reaching the Banks, our own radar was drawing a blank again, and we were alone with the squabbling birds, the colours of our containers looking vulgar and strident against the sober grey.

Then the containers, or most of the containers, disappeared. One moment we were pushing a long street of them up over the horizon, the next we were perched high over a vestigial stump of half a dozen or so. Looking down from the side of the bridge, one could just see down as far as the water, which showed as tarnished silver-foil.

Vince was the officer of the watch. '*Somewhere* on board this ship,' he said, 'there's got to be a jinx.' He lit a cigarette, and the long roll of smoke he blew inside the wheel house was cousin to the rolls of fog outside. 'We're getting a bit too much of bloody everything, this trip.'

I heard a ship sound, two or three miles off, a long muffled burp. Worried that Vince hadn't noticed this disturbingly close neighbour, I said, 'There's a ship out there . . .'

'Yeah. Us.'

I listened again. The horn was dead ahead, but sounded spookily far away.

'Women on board is always bad, of course,' Vince said. 'Rabbit's bad. Vicars are bad. I never heard anything about authors before.'

'Authors are bad.'

'I suppose it must all be meat and drink to you—hurricanes, fog, engine trouble . . . Chapter Three: "Fog on the Grand Banks". Pity we're past the iceberg season. I expect you could do with a few icebergs.'

'I was really hoping for a shipwreck. Second Officer in Heroic Mercy Dash . . . that sort of thing.'

'Yeah,' Vince grunted from the radar hood. 'The *Titanic* went down not far from here—just south of the Grand Banks.'

The fog lifted in mid-afternoon and let a few feeble rays of sunshine through. The sea was brown and dusty-looking, more inclined to take its colour from its own shallow bottom than from the distant sky. Later, after the stickies, after the Harrison Ford movie on the video, after the game of *Colditz*, I went out on to the afterdeck to clear my head and was startled by the ship's wake. For a mile at least, it stretched behind us in writhing, braided flames of phosphorescence, as brilliant as liquid steel in a smelter. The sea was swarming with microscopic life, with meganyctiphanes, dinoflagellates, noctiluca doing their dazzling thing. Slightly drunk, I clung to the rail, watching as the ship's screw went on stirring up this rich, protozoic, Grand Banks soup.

The first real sign of the United States was a close-packed archipelago of buoys marking lobster-pots or fish-traps. Around the British Isles, the standard equipment consists of a bundle of old plastic detergent bottles or a lump of tar-encrusted polystyrene, together with a length of garden cane topped by a torn rag. These buoys were smart, high-tech contrivances, freshly enamelled in scarlet, with aluminium masts and tetrahedral radar reflectors. Each buoy was flying the personal pennant of its owner, racing-yacht style. They bobbed past on the beam and danced in our wake—new, snazzy, *American* symbols.

When night fell, we caught the wink of the Nantucket light. *Almost there*. But we had lost our ridge of high pressure, and the weather was blowing up hard behind the ship, with a building swell and banks of low cloud gathering in the eastern sky. By midnight the wind was moaning round the bridge and the *Conveyor* was beginning to corkscrew in the following sea.

The telephone on Officer B's bedside table rang at four a.m. It was Captain Jackson, ringing to say that we'd passed the Ambrose lightship and that the New York pilot had just come aboard. I fought my way back into my clothes and went up to the bridge.

The city was hiding behind the low hills of Brooklyn and the thick weather. It took an age to reach the Verrazano Bridge and enter the Narrows, from where New York was suddenly on top of us. Manhattan was a dozen glittering sticks of light, through which livid storm clouds were rolling, lit from below, sooty-orange in colour, as they swirled past the middling and upper storeys of the buildings. The choppy sea in the harbour was like a lake of troubled mercury, and the water glared so fiercely that it was almost impossible to find the tiny red and green sparks of the buoys marking the deepwater channel. Then one's eye adjusted and the city's famous icons began to emerge from the general dazzle of things. *There* was Brooklyn Bridge; *there*, on her rock, was Liberty, weirdly floodlit in leprechaun green.

If the moon had crashed, the event would not have much interested the crew of the *Conveyor*, who were otherwise engaged, getting ropes out to tugs and talking into radios. With his back firmly turned on the brilliant scene to starboard, Captain Jackson was saying, 'You see, you have to keep an eye on the set of the tide in the Kill Van Kull; it's very narrow there, and there are some nasty shallow patches.'

I tried to think about the set of the tide in the Kill Van Kull, but it was no match against the scowling splendour of the illuminated city in the storm, the racing clouds, the hideous light in which

Liberty was bathed, the exaggerated sense of occasion that this moment must always have inspired. The immigrants, crowding against each other's backs, shoving and straining, must have felt that all the reports and letters home had understated the awful truth about New York. The real thing was even taller and more intimidating than the tallest story. So you looked out, numbed by the gigantism of the city, asking the immigrant's single overriding question: is there really a place *there*, for *me*?

A lice's apartment was a cell in a concrete honeycomb on East 18th Street between Gramercy Park and Union Square. I had never met Alice; I knew someone who knew her and had arranged to sub-rent her apartment, sight unseen, for two months while she was working abroad. This deal was a technical breach of the regulations of the building, so I had been told to present myself to the doormen and the super as Alice's intimate friend or at least her cousin. So far as the handicaps of sex and voice allowed, I had to be as nearly Alice herself as I could manage.

I let myself in to a neat but rather gloomy cabin, barely half the size of Officer B's—the fully furnished life of someone small, slender and dainty. Alice must once have trained in ballet and gymnastics in order to negotiate the doll's house routes and spaces of her apartment. Everything was little: little table, little chairs, little couch, little bureau, a very upright little piano with its lid open and something by Schumann on the stand. Only the bed was big: it reigned over the rest of the room from its alcove, where it was surrounded by books, angle lamps and card-index files. A patchwork animal of indeterminate species was crouched on top of the pillows. It probably had a name like Merriwether or Smudge.

Cautiously I sniffed and snooped, trying to get the measure of this rented new life. I studied the grainy framed photographs on the walls, each one inscribed 'For Alice with Love' by its photographer; a winter landscape, a woman in bed (could this be Alice herself?), a timber barn somewhere in the Far West. Alice had a serious library of modern poetry, photographic books, some stuff on Egyptology and the ancient world. No history, no politics, no obvious best sellers. There was something fierce and exclusive in her taste for Robert Lowell, Alfred Stieglitz and the Pharaohs, as if her apartment was too small to admit entry to the eccentric strangers who manage to worm their way on to most people's bookshelves.

Her kitchen—a narrow tiled slot, like a shower-stall—revealed a preference for herbal teas and decaffeinated coffee as well as a reassuring weakness for vodka and white wine. The bathroom cabinet gave nothing much away: she was prone to headaches and occasional trouble with her sinuses. I liked the smell of her shampoo.

There was a useful find on the bureau—along with a stack of snapshots, a brittle clipping from a local newspaper in Mississippi, *circa* 1954. It showed a family of small children restraining a bunch of large labrador pups, under the headline, COON-HUNTERS OF TOMORROW? The caption identified the child in the middle as Alice. The clipping, with its cosy-cute headline, was rich in tantalizing suggestions. It conjured a great white Graeco-Roman Baptist church, a segregated school where Alice would have been the clever one in the second row back, a landscape of flat cotton-fields and stands of cypress and bog-oak. There was a dusty, back-country road—Alice swinging her school bag—the lazy, grown-up talk of dogs and guns. It was all further away from New York than New York could possibly imagine—a lonely distance for anyone to travel on her own.

I ousted Smudge, or Merriwether, from the bed and tried out what it might feel like to be Alice. The last things she'd been reading were Joseph Brodsky's essays, an advanced French grammar (she still did her homework, evidently) and the October issue of *Vanity Fair*. I switched on the TV. She'd been tuned to the Cable News Network.

'Preserve your heritage of freedoms—join the National Rifle Association . . .', then the picture changed to shots of Michael Dukakis and George Bush on the presidential stump. Alice would be rooting for Dukakis, but rooting reluctantly, I guessed. She'd wince at the too-new suede zipper and too-stiff checkered leisure shirt in which he was now cajoling an audience of Iowa farmers. He kept on blinking, as if at the glare of footlights; a big-city actor trying, unsuccessfully, to pass himself off as a down-home country boy. Bush, by contrast, also somewhere out in the sticks, looked as if he'd just strolled off the golf-course: his clothes were clearly his own, and he seemed worryingly at home with the people he was talking to.

Jonathan Raban

Half attending to the garble of the candidates at my back, I lay propped on one elbow looking out through the window at Alice's view.

It was a relatively quiet corner, yet even here one could feel New York trembling under one's feet. The building shook with the wet sea-surge of the traffic as it bulleted away from the stoplight on East 18th and 3rd Avenue. In place of bird-song, there was the continuous angry warble of ambulances, patrol cars, fire-trucks. It was the sound of heart attacks and heart-break, of car crashes, hold-ups, fire-raisings, hit-and-run, flight and pursuit, sudden death; the sound of a city in a round-the-clock state of emergency. If you were going to learn to live here, you'd have to go deaf to the sound of New York and set up house in the silent bubble of your own preoccupations. For me the New York air was full of robbery and murder; for Alice, it would all be inaudible white noise. She would be placidly sitting at her piano practising scales and waiting for the kettle to come to the boil for her cup of camomile tea, snug in her cell, with uniformed guards standing watch down in the lobby. I resolved to try and learn to be like Alice.

In New York at last, the promised city, the immigrants found themselves in a cacophonic bazaar. So many *things*! The streets were awash with commodities undreamed of by the poor of Europe—new foods, smart clothes, mechanical novelties, luxuries made cheap by American techniques of mass production. Your own berth in New York might be no more than a patch of floor in a dumb-bell tenement on the Lower East Side, yet no building was so squalid that its tenants were entirely excluded from the bounty of American life. In the midst of rack-rent poverty, in conditions as bad as anything they had suffered in the old country, the immigrants would be surrounded by symbols of extravagant wealth. There were ice-cream parlours, candy stores, beef-steaks, fat cigars. In New York ordinary people, wage-earners, dined out in restaurants; they had alarm clocks and Victrola machines on which they played 'jass' music; and by the standards of Europe they were dressed like royalty.

You had a new name, assigned to you at Ellis Island by an immigration officer who was too busy to bother with the unpronounceable z's and x's of your old one. (*Gold*, because the streets of New York were supposed to be paved with the stuff, was a favourite stand-by.) You had new clothes. You might be able to speak only a word or two of English but you could still parade as a suave, fashion-conscious New Yorker.

Identity in Europe wasn't a matter of individual fancy. Even if you had the money for the materials, you couldn't dress as an aristocrat simply because you liked the look of the local noble's style. If you were Jewish, you couldn't even pass yourself off as a gentile without incurring a legal punishment. Every European was the product of a complicated equation involving the factors of lineage, property, education, speech and religion. The terms were subtle and they could be juggled: even the most rigid class system has some play in it, some room for people to move up and down within the structure. But once your personal formula had been worked out by the ruling mathematicians, the result was precise and not open to negotiation. A over B times X over Y divided by Z equalled a calico shirt, a leather jerkin and a pair of clogs.

For anyone brought up in such a system, New York must have induced a dizzying sense of social weightlessness. Here identity was not fixed by society's invisible secret police. The equation had been simplified down to a single factor—dollars.

The windows of the department stores were theatres. They showed American lives as yet unlived in, with vacant possession. When your nose was pressed hard against the glass, it was almost yours, this other life that lay in wait for you with its silverware and brocade. So you were a presser in a shirtwaist factory on Division Street, making 12.50 dollars a week—so what? The owner of the factory was your *landsman*, very nearly a cousin; he had the start on you by just a few years, and already he lived in a brownstone, uptown on 84th. Success in this city was tangible and proximate; it was all around you, and even the poorest people could smell it in the wind. The distance between slum and mansion was less than a mile; hard work . . . a lucky break . . . and you could roam through Bloomingdale's and Macy's, buying up the life you wanted to lead.

I had been to Macy's once before, in 1972, when I went foraging in the basement for a change of clothes. On a hot June afternoon the store had been blessedly cool and cavernous. The motherly assistant had made an old-fashioned fuss over my British accent, and the clothes themselves had been, by European standards, amazingly cheap. Made of some kind of acrylic stuff, they were smart, bright, all-American. I bought a striped summer jacket in synthetic seersucker, a pair of washable trousers with creases built-in and guaranteed to last for ever, two button-down shirts with white collars and blue fronts. The bill for everything came to less than seventy dollars—which, at an exchange rate of 2.40 dollars to the pound, seemed like a steal. Out on the street in my new American camouflage, I melted into the city, a regular guy at last.

Something had happened. Macy's in 1988 smelled of serious money. The air trapped in the swing-door reeked of new leather and Rive Gauche. Inside, a man in white tie and tails was rattling off popular classics on a concert grand. Above the glassy aisles and mahogany-panelled boutiques there was a heraldic blazonry of expensive trade names—Louis Vuitton, Calvin Klein, Givenchy, Dior, Ralph Lauren. It was platinum-card country; a twinkling gallery, as big as a battlefield, of gold, silk, scent and lizard-skin. When I'd last been here, there had been a slogan painted over the entrance: IT'S SMART TO BE THRIFTY. Sometime between the age of Richard Nixon and the last days of Ronald Reagan, that homely touch of American puritanism had been whitewashed over. Only frumps were thrifty now.

The crowd ran sluggishly through the long marble-pillared corridors of jewellery, handbags and cosmetics. It eddied round the girls in high heels, fish-net tights, frou-frou skirts and top hats who were squirting scent-samples at everyone, male and female, who came within their range. For a few moments, I was gridlocked with someone's reluctant husband, a tubby man wearing a bomber jacket and a leatherette helmet with earflaps, who gave off a powerful odour of sweat and attar of roses. He was hauled away, whining, to the escalators by a twin-engined Brillo pad in a fox-fur stole, while the current of the crowd bore me along into Men's Furnishings.

These 'furnishings' were disappointingly dull in themselves— plain cotton shirts, and ties that in England would be the badge of having once belonged to an obscure county regiment or minor public school. It was the way they were displayed that was extraordinary. Each counter had been converted into a grotto of evocative junk. Between the shirts and ties were piles of antique fishing rods, golf-clubs, snow-shoes, hat-boxes, tarnished silver cups, gum-boots, antlers, broken leather suitcases with labels from hotels in Split, Prague, Venice, Florence; gold-banded walking-sticks; a pair of crossed oars; a torn photograph; a battered schoolroom globe; shotgun cartridges; bits of splayed cane furniture left over from the Raj; old family snapshots in ornate silver frames.

So this was what had been in the container billed as 'bric-à-brac' on the *Conveyor*'s cargo manifest. There was a new life waiting in America for all the rubbish in the attics of genteel England. Macy's must have ransacked half the Old Rectories and Mulberry Lodges in Cheshire in order to assemble this hoard of moth-eaten Edwardiana. The rubbish apparently served some alchemical purpose: after a day or two spent in the company of a croquet mallet, a hunting flask, a box of trout flies and a pair of old stirrups, an ordinary white shirt would, I supposed, begin to stiffen with exclusiveness and nobility as it absorbed the molecules of stables, servants, log-fires, field and stream. Certainly the shirt could only justify its ninety-dollar price-tag if you were prepared to pay at least fifty dollars for the labour of the alchemist and not be over-fussy about the standard of shirt making.

The crowd poured on to the escalators. When Macy's opened in 1902, these escalators with their wood-block steps had been the latest thing; now they were of a piece with the antique luggage and the wind-up Victrola, valued the more highly for being old than being new. They rumbled up through timber-panelled shafts. We piled, hip to haunch, on to this creaky Jacob's ladder, talking in Spanish, Haitian French, Brooklyn, Russian. There was a noisy elation in the crowd, as if the act of going shopping was working like an inhalation of Benzedrine.

We climbed through a cloud bank of bras and negligées; a meadow of dresses went by. Suppose you'd just arrived from Guyana or Bucharest—here would be your vision of American plenty, the brimming cornucopia of the fruits of capitalism. Here goods queued up in line for people, not vice versa. Here you were treated as an object of elaborate cajolery and seduction.

Nothing was too much for you. At every turn of the moving staircase, Macy's had laid on a new surprise for your passing entertainment. You'd like to see the inside of an exclusive club for Victorian gentlemen? We've built one. A pioneer log cabin? Here it is. After the log cabin, a high-tech pleasure-drome of mirrors and white steel. After the pleasure-drome, a deconstructionist fantasy made of scaffolding, with banks of VDU screens all showing the same picture, of beautiful people modelling leisurewear. The whole store was wired for sound, and each architectural extravagance had its own musical signature. Duke Ellington . . . Telemann . . . Miles Davis . . . Strauss . . .

Macy's was scared stiff of our boredom. This was a world constructed for creatures with infantile attention spans, for whom every moment had to be crammed with novelties and sensations. To be so babied and beguiled, all for the sake of selling skirts and jackets, sheets and towels! It was gross, even by the relatively indulgent standards of London. Many of the people on the escalators were fresh from that other world of clothing coupons and short rations—had I been one of them, I'd have been swept by a wave of blank helplessness in the face of all this aggressive American fun.

To get by in Macy's, a sturdy sense of selfhood was required. Everything in the store whispered *for you! just for you!*—and you needed to love yourself a very great deal to live up to this continual pampering, for there was an insidious coda to the message, whispering *are you sure that* you *belong here*?

At each floor, we had to leave the escalator and walk round to the far side of the shaft; and on the way we were ingeniously tormented with mirrors, each one placed so that it appeared to be an innocuous part of the display. I kept on barging into a figure who darkly resembled Henry James's inconceivable alien. I first spotted him in the Victorian men's club: a lank and shabby character in scuffed shoes and concertina-trousers whose hair (or what little was left of it) badly needed pruning. He could have done with a new set of teeth. Had I seen him in the subway station, shaking a polystyrene cup under my nose, I'd have given him a couple of quarters and walked on fast, but in Macy's there was no escaping him. He jumped out at me from behind a rack of padlocked fur-coats, and was waiting for me at the bookstore. Wherever he was, he looked equally out of place and I grew increasingly ashamed of him.

Shame was a central part of the deal in this show. The luxurious artifice had been designed to soften you up; first, by making you feel good about yourself, then, by slugging you below the belt with a surprise punch and making you feel rotten about yourself. It worked, too. By the time I was half-way up the store, I had an American haircut and a new pair of shiny ox-blood Italian loafers. It was a pity that, though Macy's sold almost everything, they didn't seem to have a boutique where you could buy new teeth.

It was good to be back on the street, to escape this puzzling multi-storey fiction and return to the low realism of Broadway at dusk, with a hard nip in the air and a frank scowl of aggression on everyone's face as people shoved and jostled each other round the choked entrance to the subway. Two men were out of the race. One was blind and black; the other sat on a camp-stool, warbling on a bird-whistle. He held the whistle to his lips with his left hand; the sleeve of his duffel jacket was fastened with a safety pin where his right elbow should have been. There was an expression of pure benignity on his face as he trilled and fluted. His eyes were wide, their pale blue exactly matching the colour of the faded denim cap that he'd pulled down over his Harpo Marx tangle of white hair. After the elaborate cunning of Macy's approach to the retail trade, his sales-pitch was refreshingly direct. On a sheet of torn cardboard he had written in biro: BIRD WHISTLE / ALL COLORS / $1.00 EACH WHISTLE. I know a good bribe for four-year-olds when I see one and bought five whistles, in red, yellow, green, white and blue. As I picked them out of the box at the man's feet, he smiled—a big, untidy, open smile that looked as if he really meant it.

'For to make the whistle, must first to put the water in the hole!' He shook his own whistle under my nose to show me.

'Where are you from? What country?'

'Me?' he seemed surprised and pleased that anyone should ask him such a question. 'I come from Kiev. Kiev. In *Ukraine*.'

'How long in America?—how many years?'

'I come in . . . nineteen—eight-oh. I have eight years in New York.'

'What was your job in the Ukraine? What did you do before you came here?'

He grinned, sighed, blinked. 'Excuse me. Not understanding.

35

Too bad English.' His eyes, candid and friendly, remained on me as he piped a long, robin-like territorial demarcation call on his whistle. It was a disappointment—I badly wanted to know why he seemed so happy. To escape from the Soviet Union, only to find yourself hawking plastic toys on a cold Manhattan street corner, would take an extraordinarily sunny disposition if you weren't to feel ground down by your fate. But the bird-whistle man didn't seem ground down at all.

I sat in the office of Macy's Herald Square store manager, and listened to him tell a corporate rags-to-riches story. 'Before Finkelstein—' he said; in Macy's, 1974 was zero-year. *Before Finkelstein* and *After Finkelstein*.

'We were dowdy . . . old . . . declining. There was no excitement in the place. We had this dowager reputation. We were floundering—changing presidents every year, all the bad signs. We'd drifted into being a lower-end-type business.'

Then came Finkelstein, the new president of the New York division. In the manager's story, Finkelstein bore a more than glancing resemblance to another president that I could think of. He too had ridden in from the West, from Macy's California, and he was credited with having made Macy's people feel proud once again to belong to Macy's.

It was Finkelstein who erased the sign saying that it was smart to be thrifty. 'Before Finkelstein, Macy's was just a store for moderates.'

'Moderates?'

'Moderates. Moderate income, moderate spenders. The "less affluent".'

I liked the sinisterly Orwellian flavour of the word.

'Now we look to hit the upper echelon.'

Finkelstein had begun to 'lose the moderates' by emptying the bargain basement for which Macy's had been famous. In its place he had installed The Cellar, an arcade of glassed-in boutiques where you could buy 'French' bread, hand-made chocolates, espresso machines, fondue sets, chafing dishes, canteens of silver cutlery and 'gourmet' hampers. *Before Finkelstein*, the ground floor had been occupied by counters of candy, drugs and notions; *After*, it was given over to scent, scarves and handbags, along with concert pianists and girls in tights and top hats. On the upper floors, he weeded out the jeans and cheap acrylics and brought in the big rag trade names—the Calvin Kleins, Giorgio Armanis, Ralph Laurens.

Macy's went on selling a lot of inexpensive, functional things that couldn't be found in grander places like Bloomingdale's or Bonwit Teller; but they were increasingly relegated to the further reaches of the building, on floors a long ride away by escalator.

'Dealing with the moderate customer, it's not a problem where to place your merchandise. The moderate, she'll go out there and *find* it.'

Finkelstein, who had himself grown up in the New York suburb of La Rochelle, where his father had been an egg-and-butter merchant, had the measure of the city. It was an astute decision to take Macy's 'upscale', even though the store stood in what was now one of the seediest quarters of midtown Manhattan, on the rat run between Times Square and Penn Station; an area of welfare hotels, beggary, purse-snatching and addiction. Macy's main rival for the moderate trade was Gimbel's, a spit away on the south side of 34th Street; and Gimbel's stuck with the moderates. For ten years, its business steadily crumbled. By the beginning of Reagan's second term, Gimbel's was holding desperate one-day sale after one-day sale in a last ditch effort to regain its customers. Finally it went bust.

There was no percentage in moderates any more. No self-regarding moderate wanted to be treated *as* a moderate; and Finkelstein set about lapping his customers in the illusion, at least, of aristocratic luxury.

The stages of this exercise in social mountaineering could be tracked in the changing language of the store's advertising. In 1933, for instance, a mail-order catalogue set out the Macy philosophy in the penny-plain terms that marked out Macy's from all the other New York department stores:

> We sell only for cash. Resulting economies including efficiency and volume save, we estimate, six per cent. We endeavor to have the prices of our merchandise reflect this saving, subject to limitations over which we have no control.

In the early seventies, just before Finkelstein, the underlying tone was still the same, even if the phrasing was a great deal snappier:

CAST YOUR THRIFTY EYE OVER BARGAINS YOU'LL FIND HARD
TO BELIEVE! (*Christmas catalogue, 1970*)

Captain Rowland H. Macy believed in bargains 113 years
ago when he started Macy's. We still do! (*Christmas
catalogue, 1971*)

It took the advertising department a little while to catch up with
Finkelstein's style of doing things. In their 1977 catalogue for The
Cellar—once the bargain basement—they hit on a language of
expensive golden words:

Come on down to where the four corners of the world
meet in a bustling melange of shops. A Marketplace with
wares to tempt the palate, titillate the senses. From
succulent delicacies to old world confections. A quaint
Apothecary . . .

So it went on—with little dabs of French, self-conscious archaisms,
bursts of indulgent alliteration. Yet this was restrained by
comparison with the catalogue of 1988. *Think Status* . . . it said:

Wrap her in tapestry . . . Mark Cross leathergoods
collection, patterned for success, to carry her through her
busy day . . . Princess Gardner solar calculator clutch.
Karung lizard embossed leather . . . Baccarat, the
crystal of kings, once reserved for royalty. Hare
sculpture, especially for animal lovers, $69.00 . . . Lace
and silk charmeuse gown . . . Judith Leiber's jeweled
goldtone monkey. A work of art that just happens to be a
handbag . . .

This last—and most peculiar-looking—object cost 1,980 dollars.
Even the most pedestrian goods were painted over with words
designed to associate them with royalty, antiquity, exotic zoology,
art. What would have been a 'line' was now a 'collection', and the
vocabulary of the art museum was borrowed by the copywriters to
give the merchandise the glow of 'timeless' (a favourite word)
value. Brand names were now artists' signatures, and everything
possible was done to suggest that the personal hand of the designer
had 'crafted' each individual commodity in the line. In an unwitting

echo of Karl Marx's theory of value-as-labour, the advertising men of Macy's invited you to buy, not a dress or a handbag, but 'a work'.

People in New York evidently kept their children locked in closets or hidden in secret attics. For weeks, I'd been moving in what seemed to be a childless city. The six or seven children I'd met—and equipped with bird-whistles—had themselves been as rare as golden orioles.

Now, on Thanksgiving Day, the children were out of the closet. As I walked across Central Park at breakfast time, it seemed as if a whole generation had mysteriously sprouted overnight. There were children in strollers, children perched aloft on fathers' shoulders, babes in arms, children on tricycles, in gangs, in orderly crocodiles, every infant muffled to the ears against the icy brilliance of the morning. For once, the harsh and rascally air of New York had a wholesome smell of candy, milk and cookies.

There was a religiose flavour to the language in which Macy's Thanksgiving Day parade was spoken of within the store. It was Macy's way of Reaching Out and of Serving the Community. It was also the store's most famous advertisement: broadcast live on national television, the parade announced the beginning of the Christmas shopping season. The parade was a spectacular endorsement of Macy's special claim to be 'a family store'. It underpinned the wording of the jingles that were broadcast several times a day on local radio and television: *'Macy's! Macy's! We're a part of your life!'* and its variant, *'Macy's! Macy's! Now more than ever, you're a part of my life!'*

In every apartment overlooking the parade route, there was a party. I was bound for a tenth floor co-op on Central Park West. It was packed to the seams with pale and scholarly looking children holding glasses of orange juice like cocktails and shooting the breeze about the respective merits of their nursery schools.

They broke cover to a cry of 'Garfield!' as the first battalion of the parade, with its gas-filled dirigibles, floats and marching bands, came heading our way. A creature, famous to them but not to me, swayed above the tree-tops in giant, inflated effigy, then loomed at our window, its whiskers on a level with the balcony. Far down below, a team of a dozen or more burly winch-men was needed to keep the thing tethered to the ground. They hauled and pumped on their ropes, and when a flutter of wind came through the park, a man was lifted clean off the Tarmac as the balloon reached for the sky. There was a rapture on the balcony. 'Big Bird!' 'Superman!' 'Woodstock!' 'Snoopy!'

The Radio City Rockettes went past—a band of girl hussars from Pennsylvania—a troop of clowns—a tumble of acrobats. Here came the statue of Liberty in painted polystyrene . . . and there were the Pilgrim Fathers in stove-pipe hats. The Minute Men of Lexington had brought their muskets, and a three-masted ship, all guns firing, blasting the crowds with paper streamers, turned out, a shade surprisingly, to be the *Mayflower*. Most of the floats had a throne, on which sat a real, live New York eminence. The children beside me named these people. A TV weatherman was being cheered down the length of Central Park West as if he was personally responsible for the dazzling sunshine.

'He pitches for the Mets.'

I pointed out the woman in furs who was riding on the front of the statue of Liberty. I held out a distant hope that she might be Bess Myerson. 'Who's that?'

'Oh that's . . . just some celebrity.'

'Is Mayor Koch anywhere?'

'Mayor *Koch*?—if he came, they'd *throw* things at him,' said a cynical seven-year-old.

The religiose language had more point than I had given it credit for. The Thanksgiving Day parade was the secular, American descendant of the European Catholic Easter procession in which all the icons and saints' bones are removed from the churches and carried ceremonially around the town. The baseball hero, the gaseous, rubbery Mickey Mouse, the *Mayflower* pilgrims were the totems and treasured relics of a culture, as the New Orleans jazz and Sousa marches were its solemn music. Here was America going by.

RIAN MALAN

MSINGA

1

The road to Msinga begins in white South Africa and runs for hours through neat and orderly white farm land, not so different in appearance from parts of central California. Some ten miles beyond the last white town, you cross the border between the First and Third Worlds, between white South Africa and black kwaZulu. The border isn't marked; there is no need. You know you are coming into a different country, a different world. The white centreline vanishes, and the road itself starts rearing and plunging, like a turbulent river rushing towards a waterfall. The very mood of the landscape changes. And then you round a bend, and the tar falls away beneath the wheels, and you're looking down into Africa, into a vast, sweltering valley strewn with broken hills, mud huts, and tin-roofed shanties. From the rim of the escarpment, it looks as though some mad god has taken a knife to the landscape, slashing ravines and erosion gulleys into its red flesh and torturing its floor into rugged hills. This is Msinga, a magisterial district in the self-governing homeland of kwaZulu, the place of Zulus.

As white South Africa fell away behind me, the countryside grew barren and dusty. There were no fences. Goats and cattle strayed into the road. The deeper I drove into Msinga, the worse it got: less grass, less hope, more goats and more hopeless black people sitting motionless as stones in the roadside dust. The place was an ecological Hiroshima. The last big trees looked like mangroves, stranded high and dry by a receding tide of soil. The earth at their feet had washed away down gaping erosion gulleys and into the river, leaving the first nine inches of root dangling in thin air. In some places, there was no soil at all, just sheets of grey slate and clayey subsoil baked hard as concrete by the sun. Thermals rising from these zones of devastation caused such turbulence at 30,000 feet that white businessmen jetting between Johannesburg and Durban were losing their lunch over Msinga. South African Airways solved the problem by rerouting its flights. That was white South Africa's usual response to Msinga's problems: Avoid them.

Whites couldn't bear to look at Msinga because its devastation was to some large extent their own fault. Msinga was declared a location, or Zulu reservation, in 1849. As early as 1878, government reports were noting that it was dry, barren and prone to famine. In the century since, the district's population had quintupled to maybe 120,000, the natural increase augmented in the late 1960s by 22,000 'surplus people'—blacks cleared off nearby white farm land and dumped across the border in kwaZulu. The land was carrying at least twice as many humans, cattle and goats as it could support. That is why it was turning into desert.

Some twenty miles inside the district, a dirt road peeled off the tar and headed north along the banks of the Tugela River. It was a bucking, boulder-strewn abomination of a road, and at the end of it lay an agricultural development project called Mdukatshani, Place of Lost Grasses, where a man named Neil Alcock had done his last good works. As I bounced through the project's gate a Zulu man wearing tattered overalls and huge coloured discs in his ear-lobes leaped out to challenge me. After checking me out, he set off at a trot down the track, beckoning me to follow. A few hundred yards farther on, he ordered me to park, led me through a wooden gate and into a thicket of thorn trees. Then he saluted and disappeared.

I was left standing on a bluff about twenty feet above the muddy Tugela River. It was dusk, almost dark. A vervet monkey was tethered in the tree above my head. Peering into the surrounding gloom, I realized I was standing in front of a house of sorts. It was made of mud and thatched with grass. A gnarled old tree rose up through the floor, poked its limbs through the walls and soared into the darkening sky. The house was the colour of the landscape, of rock and grass and dust, and virtually invisible in the half-light. Instead of windows, there were holes in the walls and the doors and shutters were made of raw logs. The walls were plastered with smooth red mud and the furniture was all stone. Long slabs of grey slate served as benches and tables, and some large boulders, polished smooth by the river, were offered as chairs. It was the Flintstones' living-room, save for an incongruous plastic telephone.

The river rushed past this extraordinary structure, turned sharply to the left and emptied into a still pool at the base of a cliff. Something was moving down there, on a shelf of flat rock beside the pool. At first, I took it to be a troop of baboons drinking from the river, but the creatures scattered and came towards me, revealing themselves to be a woman and her dogs. A white woman, some forty years old. She came loping up the footpath on powerful calves, a curtain of straight blond hair waving to and fro across her face. She was wearing an old cotton dress and a threadbare cardigan. Her bare calves were criss-crossed with thorn scratches. Her face, when she finally lifted it, was somehow medieval—perfectly oval, with a high, broad forehead and oval eyes, all framed by blond hair that fell to her shoulders from a middle parting. She was spectrally thin. The hand she offered was horny with callus and the accompanying look was disconcertingly cool.

This was Creina, Neil Alcock's widow, a woman of formidable and fearful repute. Awed Zulus in the surrounding hills whispered that she was a *sangoma*, or witch-doctor, and whites in the cities throught she was insanely brave to live the way she did, alone in a lawless and dangerous place. I had been warned that she didn't suffer fools, gawkers or sensation-seeking reporters, whom she referred to as 'looters'. When I first called to ask if I could visit, she said, 'We have a rule here, Mr Malan. We only allow visitors who bring tangible benefits to the valley.' I offered to bring a pick-up truckful of corn and she laughed scornfully. 'We can't be bought either,' she said. In the end, though, she relented, at least to the extent of allowing me to present my case in person.

So Creina Alcock made me a cup of coffee, sat me down outside the door of her hut and invited me to explain myself. By now, the sun had set and it was bitterly cold and dark. I suspected she was hoping I'd be so uncomfortable that I'd get into my car and return to white South Africa, but I stuck it out—not that I thought it very likely that she would talk to me. Her late husband was a famous liberal, you see. In Neil Alcock's lifetime, Mdukatshani had been a station on the South African *via dolorosa*, a place where foreign diplomats and journalists came for a first-hand look at the misery of life in the tribal homelands. I had collected a file of newspaper clippings date-lined Msinga and they constituted about as withering an indictment of apartheid as I had ever read. The Zulus of Msinga were desperately poor and downtrodden. There were no jobs and the ravaged land would no longer yield enough food to support a family. Msinga's men spent their lives in labour barracks in distant cities; its women and children spent their lives waiting. In Msinga, a husband or father was someone you saw once a year and for that you counted yourself lucky. If your bread-winner got fired, injured on the job, or died, you faced starvation.

In many ways, then, Msinga was the ultimate apartheid horror story and the Alcocks themselves were always good for a side-bar. They had spent two decades living among Africans, like Africans, trying to undo some of the harm done by apartheid. They lived in mud huts and shat in holes in the ground. They washed their clothes and bodies in the Tugela River and drank its muddy water. Visitors found flies and ants in the sugar-bowl and boiled tadpoles in their coffee. The Alcocks were always dusty and dishevelled. They endured fire ants in their armpits and rats in their beds, unbearable heat in summer and biting cold in winter. They were as ragged as the black peasants among whom they worked, and thinner to boot. They were the only whites in the country who lived beyond all suspicion of complicity. In a way, Neil Alcock had given his life to his cause, and his death was marked by an obituary in the London *Times*—a rare honour indeed for a South African.

I somehow doubted that the widow of such a man would be receptive to the dark things I was thinking and feeling about South Africa. I thought of lying and telling her I had come to investigate apartheid atrocities, like all the others before me, but I was tired of lying, so I told the truth. I told her I was searching for a way to live in this strange country—for an alternative, if one existed, to the law of my Afrikaner ancestor Dawid Malan, as formulated on the far bank of the Great Fish River. I observed that she and Neil seemed to have crossed a similar river and penetrated deeper into Africa than any other whites in our time. 'I want to know,' I concluded, 'what you have learned here.' And then I sat back, expecting to be asked to leave.

Instead, Creina fell silent for a long time, so long I thought she'd fallen asleep. When she finally spoke, it was to pose a series of penetrating questions. She asked whether I believed in truth, and sought to serve it honourably. She asked what sins I had committed in my life and what I understood by the word *love*. She threw out quotes from D. H. Lawrence and T. S. Eliot and kept asking what I thought. I thought I was hallucinating. I was sitting outside a mud hut on a pitch-dark night in the heart of the Dark Continent being riddled by a sphinx. She seemed to be guarding some secret, some treasure, and testing me to see whether I was worthy of receiving it, whether I understood the gravity of my own question. I answered to the best of my ability and she lapsed into silence again. In the end, the widow Alcock decided to sleep on it. She produced a flashlight, led me up a dark footpath and into the mud hut kept ready for guests.

It was very cold that night. The chill crept in through the hut's open doorway, through the chinks between the mud walls and the thatched roof. The instant I snuffed out the candle, something came in from outside and started skittering around the floor. Next, it was rooting around inside my bag. It skittered again and then it was on the bed. A rat, by the weight of it. I flung it off me and relighted the candle, but the creature was nowhere to be seen, so I pulled the blankets over my head and fell asleep. In the course of the night, I was twice woken up by the pitter-patter of tiny feet across my face. I surged up, shouting and yelling, but the rat wouldn't go away. It was utterly fearless, or maybe it was just desperate. In winter, everything and everyone in Msinga grew desperate.

In the morning, there was a pail of water and a washing bowl at my bedside, but I decided I'd rather stink than wash in the bitter cold. A hole in the ground behind my hut led down to an underground chamber, in the centre of which stood a 'long drop'—a plastic toilet on a wooden platform suspended above a deep pit of shit. This throne was surrounded by cobwebs and the walls were full of holes and crannies that surely harboured snakes. After pissing, I walked down to the river to brush my teeth. Frost crunched beneath my boots. The muddy water was so cold that it numbed my face, sent shocks racing up my fillings and into my brain. I'd been in Msinga barely twelve hours and I was already thinking: How the fuck does she stand this?

I found Creina in the open-air kitchen behind her house, boiling water on a gas cooker. She made coffee and we drank it on a stone patio above the river. The sun rose from behind a twin-humped mountain called Mashunka and its first rays turned the tawny flood-plain across the river into a wash of gold. The river curved away in a series of still pools, each veiled by mist. The valley was very beautiful in the early light. It was a landscape, as Creina put it, of 'enormous dramatic potential'.

Over the years, she and Neil had often sat here at night, listening to gunfire in the hills and watching tracers arcing across the sky. A few years earlier, the Zulu people living on one of Mashunka's twin humps had fought a war against those on the other. After that, the people on the larger hump went to war against the people of the valley beyond. I drained my tin mug and discovered a dreg of river mud at the bottom. A very strange place indeed.

After a while, the sun acquired some strength and movement returned to my numb limbs. I guess it must have warmed my cold blood, too, because I just didn't have the heart to ask the first question on my mind. I wanted to ask: Where is it? Where is the agricultural development? What have you accomplished here? What did Neil die for? I was expecting to see tilled fields, fenced paddocks, barns and tractors. Instead, there was nothing but a cluster of mud buildings, the ruin of a water-wheel and the lone and level bush stretching far away.

So I alluded and insinuated, and Creina answered with aphorisms about Africa, about how slow it was to change, how the chameleon wavers with each step, how any change is so slow as to be imperceptible, and so deep as to be virtually immeasurable. Eventually, she seemed to lose patience with me. She suggested we take a walk, so I could get a better feel for this place in which she lived.

The project's land began at the river, crossed over a range of hills and stretched away across the plain beyond. It was dry, rugged country, riven by deep dongas and choked with thickets of thorn trees. I followed Creina along a footpath that led away from the river and up into the hills. She stopped occasionally to exclaim over a rare plant or to point out a patch of *rooigras*, 'red grass'. In these parts, she said, there are many grasses, but the red grass is king, so sweet and tasty to cattle that it is the first species to disappear when the land is overgrazed and the last to return. These few stands of red grass were one step of the African chameleon, one sign that the land was healing. The tendrils of grass growing in the bed of a nearby donga were another. It took nature 70,000 years to create an inch of soil, she said, so it would take aeons for this land to heal completely.

That was my botany lesson. Its moral was: Be patient. At the top of the hills, my history lesson commenced. Beyond lay an endless plain of grassland and thornbush, so rugged that it took hours to cross the first two miles of it. This was the plain of Ngongolo, site of the country's last great tribal battle, fought in 1944 by 8,000 Thembu and Mchunu armed mostly with spears and shields. Seventy-six men died in that battle, fighting for land that had belonged to whites, at least on paper, since 1849.

This land had once been a 'kaffir farm', you see, a labour farm. Indeed, all the land around us, as far as the eye could see, had belonged to labour farmers—absentee white landlords who usually lived on sugar or wattle plantations in more fertile regions. Such men had need of many labouring hands in certain seasons, so they bought land on the borders of the African tribal reserves and allowed blacks to live on it. In return, they extracted six months' labour from every man on the property, sometimes from his wives and children, too. Otherwise, the blacks were left entirely to their own devices. They lived in the traditional manner, under the rule of tribal chiefs. They worked the land, grazed their cattle on it and buried the fathers whom they worshipped in its red earth. They even fought wars over it, as in 1944. In their hearts and minds, it was their land.

As far as white liberals were concerned, the six-month system reeked of feudalism, so they agitated for its abolition. In 1969, the apartheid government bowed to mounting pressure and outlawed labour farming, leaving hundreds of thousands of black labour tenants stranded inside 'white' South Africa, making a complete mess of the grand apartheid master plan. Pretoria decided that most of them had to go back to where they 'belonged', back to the tribal homelands.

Elsewhere, labour tenants left quietly. In this area, though, on the land where Creina and I were walking, the Zulus dug in their heels and refused to go. So the police moved in and rounded them up at gunpoint. Huts were torched, stragglers hunted down with helicopters. Thousands of people were put on government trucks, driven over the causeway at Tugela Estates and dumped in the desolation of Msinga. It was as though a great wave had swept the Zulu off the land and dumped them like hurricane debris on the far side of the border, where there was no free land for them to farm and no room for their cattle. God knows how they were meant to survive. Perhaps they weren't expected to survive at all. They were officially known as surplus people, anyway.

When they first came to Msinga, Creina told me, she and Neil had walked this path with an ancient Zulu man, one of the thousands driven off the land in the forced removals. The old man was overcome with emotion. In his heart, this land was his land and he had never thought to see it again. He greeted every tree by name, Creina told me, and when they reached the largest tree on all the plain, he sat down in its shade and said: 'All my fatigue lies buried under this tree.'

Beyond the old man's tree, we turned west and fought our way down the brush-choked walls of the Skhelenge Gorge. When the Alcocks first came to Msinga, a skeletal black man was living in a cave in its sunless depths. His name was Delanie Mbatha and he had temporarily lost his sanity when the police drove him off his ancestral land. He thought to himself: This is a terrible country, where white men do such things. I must leave, he thought. So he put his belongings into a sack and set out on foot, looking for another country.

Delanie had never seen an atlas and had no idea where he was going. He walked all the way to East London, about 700 miles away. In East London, black people spoke a different language, but everything was otherwise the same. It was still South Africa. There was no escape. So Delanie turned around and walked all the way back to Msinga. He wanted to be close to the shades of his forefathers, so he moved into a cave in the depths of the gorge, where he lived on roots, ants and spiders and waited for the world to end.

Beyond Delanie's cave, Creina and I climbed out of the gorge. Creina sat down on a rock on the brink of a precipice and started peeling an orange. I was too tired and dusty to ask any more stupid questions and I suppose that is what she intended. She invited me to sit down beside her and started talking.

2

Neil Alcock was born in a stone farm cottage in 1919 and grew up to own a farm of his own. It was called Sunset and lay in the foothills of the Drakensberg Mountains, where the streams were so clear, cold and clean that trout survived in them. Neil Alcock had some sort of learning disability and had struggled in school. He was a gifted farmer, though. He knew the names of all the plants and grasses, all the animals and birds. He understood the ways of nature and the interdependence of living things. He took good care of his land and in time prospered greatly. By the mid-1950s, he had built a fine house on Sunset and installed in it a pretty wife, who bore two children, a boy and a girl, both of whom attended the right 'public' schools. Neil Alcock was a leading member of the local Farmers' Association and a Freemason to boot.

Outwardly, all that really distinguished him from his white neighbours was his uncanny way with cattle—he could calm a calving cow simply by laying a hand on its head—and the way he treated his 'boys', his African labourers. He allowed them to run their own cattle on his range and granted each man eight acres to farm on his own account. If their chiefs or headmen called on him, he fed them at his own table, off his own china, and gave them beds with sheets in his own house, just as if they were white. And then he joined Alan Paton's Liberal Party and proceeded to sign up all the unwashed 'boys' in the district as members. In rural Natal in the 1950s, such behaviour was virtually certifiable, but whites tended to accept it as a queer eccentricity in a man they otherwise respected.

Neil Alcock was a liberal, but never soft or sentimental, you see. He never preached or moralized. If anyone asked why he stood for democracy, he muttered: 'Everyone has the right to make their own mistakes.' Beyond that, he was a man of action. He could run barefoot across mountain ranges, swim swollen rivers and nurse crippled Land Rovers across trackless swamps. He could fix almost any engine and make ingenious contraptions from spare parts. 'Nothing that can't talk can beat me,' he boasted.

Nor could most men. Anyone who crossed the young Neil Alcock got 'ten kinds of living shit knocked out of them', in his eldest son David's phrase. He wasn't a bully, though, and his violence was never unjust. He simply hadn't mastered the civilized arts of compromise and appeasement. If something was wrong, it had to be set right, by any means necessary. If circumstances demanded it, Neil Alcock would plant himself in the path of a thundering train. That is exactly what he did when sparks from a passing steam-engine set fire to grasslands near his home: chased the train down, parked his car across the tracks and informed the astounded engineer that he was under arrest.

This is an image of Neil Alcock we must hold in our minds: a man with thunderbolts of anger in his eyes, facing down a train because that was the right thing to do. In a country where so much was wrong, that attitude was a lethal liability. Sooner or later, Neil Alcock was doomed to run into a wrong too profound to be set right. As it turned out, he encountered it in a brimming milk-pail in the late 1950s.

At the time, he was still living the sweet life of an ordinary white farmer, cushioned and cosseted by government loans, price supports and subsidies. His prosperity was based on milk, which he sold—at a heavily subsidized price—to the government Milk Board. In the late fifties, the milk market glutted and the Milk Board started dumping its surplus into the sea, to keep prices up. Meanwhile, black South Africans had one of the highest mortality rates in the world, largely because they didn't have enough food to eat. Millions of blacks seldom saw milk, because they were too poor to buy it at the retail price.

To Neil Alcock, this seemed wrong. Milk was meant to be drunk, not dumped. So he put a milk-can on the back of a bicycle and sent one of his labourers into Pholela to see whether the blacks wanted to buy it at cost. The Zulu returned to say that his people were very grateful, and would the master please send more cheap milk? The next day, Neil put the milk on a truck and drove over to Pholela himself, and that was the end of his first life. He had opened the door into another world, and he was sucked through it, into a vortex of hopelessness and need.

Pholela was a 'homeland' and South Africa's homelands were desperately sorry places. When whites first asserted control over the land in the mid-nineteenth century Africans were confined to reservations barely large enough to support existing populations. By 1960, the homelands were overflowing, overgrazed and overploughed to the brink of ecological devastation. Some 7,000,000 Africans were still trying to practice traditional subsistence agriculture on their ruined land, and most were close to starving.

In Pholela, as elsewhere, four in ten children died in infancy. Many of those who survived were dulled or deformed by kwashiorkor or rickets. Their mothers were often sickly and dry-breasted, their fathers riddled with tuberculosis.

Under the circumstances, it seemed obscene that surplus milk should be thrown into the sea, so Neil started selling his entire production at cost to the poor people of Pholela. Demand exceeded supply, so he started buying up his white neighbours' surplus, too. Soon, he was calling white dairy farmers all over the province, saying: 'I am the sea; dump your milk on me.' Eventually, even that wasn't enough, so he went to Johannesburg and persuaded some wealthy white philanthropists to bankroll a nationwide surplus-distribution scheme. He called this new organization Kupugani, Zulu for Raise Yourself, and left his farm to run it. He travelled the country sponging up agricultural surplus in white South Africa and setting up centres to distribute it at cost to hungry blacks.

Wherever he went, Neil encountered misery and hunger— more misery and hunger than he had ever imagined. So he spoke out. Liberal English newspapers started running black-bordered articles headlined: STARVATION: A NATIONAL DISGRACE. The secret police started tailing Neil wherever he went, trying to link him to imaginary communist plots. Some whites accused him of interfering with the balance of nature, arguing that blacks were breeding too fast and that the 'surplus' should be allowed to die off. Others were shamed. Beatnik folk-singers staged benefits for Kupugani and guilt-stricken liberals dug deep into their pockets. Flash bulbs detonated, donations poured in and Neil Alcock became something of a household name. When a white newspaper invited readers to nominate a public figure to go to America and meet Elizabeth Taylor as part of some Hollywood publicity stunt, Neil Alcock came in second.

He wasn't entirely immune to glamour, but he didn't take his new celebrity very seriously.

Whatever good Kupugani had done wasn't enough. It was barely even a beginning. Like many whites who achieved consciousness, Neil started choking on the privileges of whiteness. His salary seemed too great in a country where so many had so little, so he gave it away or ploughed it back into Kupugani. Then he shed the life-style. He refused to sleep in segregated hotels or eat in segregated restaurants. Within a year, he had become a wandering ascetic, sleeping on roadsides, subsisting on milk and army-surplus fortified biscuits. He went into debt and eventually lost his farm. After that, he lost his wife and chidren, too. By the time Creina met him, he owned nothing but an old Peugeot station-wagon, a blackened cooking pot and a dog named Ulysses, in recognition of his broad travels.

At the time, Creina Bond was in her early twenties and working as a newspaper reporter in the Pietermaritzburg bureau of Durban's *Daily News*. She was one of the more sought-after women in the city's smart young set, the blond and beautiful escort of famous sportsmen and yachtsmen. She was a serious girl at heart, though, with little stomach for the sweet white life. Like many reporters on the English newspapers, Creina was thirsting to strike blows for the cause, to 'do something' about apartheid, or at least to write about the suffering it was causing. In 1963, she heard that Kupugani's famous monk penitent was living in the back of his station-wagon on the outskirts of her city. She shared Neil's interests in nature and ecology, and in the homeland hunger problem, so she badgered her bureau chief into sending her along on one of his expeditions into the wounded African heartland.

They set off on a weekday morning, Neil, Creina and her sister Joey crammed into the front seat of the clattering old Peugeot. In the flesh, Neil Alcock was a striking man—six feet three inches tall, thin, wiry and balding now that he was in his forties. His head was curiously elongated toward the crown, giving him the look of the African bird called *hamerkop*, or 'hammerhead'. His face was the face of a bird of prey, long and thin, with a hooked nose, jutting brow and furiously beetling eyebrows. People who knew him by reputation were surprised to find that he wasn't at all sanctimonious in person. The eyes behind his dusty spectacles were full of humour and kindness. He laughed a lot, made jokes at his own expense and told spellbinding stories about Africa.

Within hours of their meeting, Creina concluded that Neil Alcock was an extraordinary man, the only white she had ever met who was completely at ease in the world of Africans. That first night, he introduced her to Gatsha Buthelezi, an obscure young Zulu nobleman who was about to start his rise to power and prominence. Buthelezi threw his arms around the white man, greeting him as 'my brother'. He and Neil sat up late into the night, talking politics in fluent Zulu. The following day, Neil's party pressed on into Tongaland, a wild region near the Mozambique border. Wherever they went, the same thing happened; black leaders threw their arms around the white man and called him brother. In a country where almost all dealings across the racial gulf were poisoned by awkwardness and condescension, Neil's relationship with blacks was loose, easy and completely natural.

Between stops, Neil talked about Africa and its fragile ecology. He had never made it beyond tenth grade in school, but he was a profoundly wise man, especially when it came to land and soil and the peculiar problems of peasant farmers in Africa. He was convinced that the people of South Africa's tribal homelands would ultimately starve if they were not helped to conserve soil and increase crop yields. 'This is our worst problem,' he would say. 'It is worse than apartheid, because it will be harder to solve.' He made Creina think and he also seemed to have a destiny. For a serious girl, that was an irresistible combination. And so, when Neil asked her to marry him, she did, in spite of her famly's initially strenuous objections. She was twenty-three; Neil, forty-six.

They wanted to hold the ceremony in the bush, in some wild and African place. South Africa had a law against open-air weddings, though, so they had to get married in a church. They were planning to serve champagne at the reception, but there was a law against that, too. Many of the guests were Africans, and Africans weren't allowed to drink white man's liquor. The law kept a close eye on Neil Alcock, so his wedding reception was dry. The guest of honour was the novelist Alan Paton and Neil's best man was the Zulu chieftain Gatsha Buthelezi. All this was so wildly unusual, in South Africa in 1965, that the pictures made the front page of newspapers in distant Johannesburg.

The Alcocks spent the first year of their marriage living in a car and the next ten years in an abandoned chicken and rabbit run on a Roman Catholic mission farm, where Neil had set up an agricultural demonstration project. The mission was overgrazed, badly eroded, teeming with hungry people and perfect for Neil's purposes. He had come to heal it, you see, to show homeland Africans how it could be done.

He began by convincing local Africans to exchange direct ownership of their cows for pieces of paper representing shares in an intangible cattle co-operative. This was no small thing. A piece of paper was not a cow and in an African cattle culture a man without cows was no man at all. In the end, though, the suspicious peasants agreed to give Neil's plan a try and black Africa's first cattle co-operative came into being.

Once the cattle were pooled into a single herd, it became possible to fence the communal land and rotate the livestock from camp to camp, allowing the grass to recover. Financed by a grant from the Chairman's Fund, charity arm of the gold- and diamond-mining Anglo-American Corporation, Neil set the jobless to work, blocking gulleys with stones and thorn bushes. In time, the wounds in the land started healing. Grass returned to the hillsides, and dry springs came back to life. As the grazing recovered, the communal herd doubled in size. On a continent where most development projects failed, all this was something of a miracle. Development workers came from far and wide to stare at the mission's lush pastures and fat cattle and to replenish their sense of what was possible.

They found the Alcocks still living in a hovel—an abandoned Trappist winery that had been a chicken and rabbit run prior to their arrival. The Alcocks shat in a long drop and had no running water. They ate vegetables and *putu* and read by lamplight. They owned little but a few books and some changes of clothing. They had two sons by now, G. G. and Rauri, little sandy-haired boys who spoke English with a Zulu inflection, saying 'tlee' instead of 'three' and 'volovolo' instead of 'revolver'. As managing director of an entity known as Church Agricultural Projects, or CAP, Neil was entitled to a salary of about seventy-five dollars a month, but he never drew it. Creina was editing a small magazine called *African Wildlife* by mail. The job paid fifty dollars a month, about what a domestic servant would earn in one of Johannesburg's better suburbs, but it was enough for a family of four to live on, if they lived like blacks. Neil was widely thought of as a visionary, a guru, even a secular saint.

A saint? Father Barney was not so sure about that. Father Barney was one of the Franciscan priests who ministered to the mission folk's spiritual needs. He was an Irishman and in his cups was wont to say that apartheid was nothing as compared with the misery the British had inflicted on the Irish. Father Barney and his fellow clergymen disapproved of Neil's divorce and were distressed to learn that Creina was agnostic. When she was caught dispensing birth-control pills to black women, the fathers' worst fears were confirmed. 'Some of them aren't even married!' one priest sputtered. The priests declared war on the Alcocks and a long and bitter struggle ensued. The Holy Fathers won. Citing his desire to preserve 'the Catholic character of the mission', the archbishop of Natal declined to renew Neil's co-operative's lease when it expired.

And so in the winter of 1975, Neil Alcock and his local Zulu lieutenants saddled horses and drove the co-op's cattle off the mission farm. His most generous backer, the Chairman's Fund, had offered to help buy a new home for the project. It was a huge spread, 6,000 acres of unfenced, undeveloped and badly eroded land. It lay sixty miles away, across the river from the place called Msinga.

3

Msinga is . . . Oh, God, how do I explain Msinga? Msinga is wild and yet it is not leaping with buck and lions. There is probably not a single antelope left alive in the entire valley. The district is criss-crossed by tar roads and power lines, packed with tin-roofed shanties and mud huts. It is a place of head-spinning contrasts. In Msinga, you see black men driving goats and black men driving BMWs. You see Zulu women going down on all fours at the feet of nondescript old men in ill-fitting three-piece suits; they are tribal chiefs or headmen and must be shown respect. You see bare-breasted Zulu maidens with shaved heads and bodies draped with beads. They seem to have stepped out of *National Geographic*, but if you look closer you see that they're wearing Day-Glo leg-warmers and running shoes. You see men in traditional dress carrying briefcases through the bush, and school-uniformed teenagers dancing through the wastelands with ghetto-blasters on their shoulders. So Msinga isn't quaint and it's not storybook Africa. It is a sprawling rural slum, infested with dope-smugglers, gun-runners and bandits. It is the Iron Age shat squalling and sullen into the twentieth century. Its people look broken as they eat the dust of your passing car, but in their hearts they are proud and untamed and utterly ungovernable by anyone.

It's easy to blame the apartheid regime for Msinga's misery, but Nelson Mandela or Fidel Castro might not have done any better. The district capital, Tugela Ferry, is an indescribably forlorn and dusty little hamlet on the banks of the Tugela River. From its rooftops, you look out over a broad flood-plain. A network of gravity canals comes snaking out down the distant hills and fans out across the plain. These canals draw irrigation water from the Tugela eight miles upstream, carry it across the plain, past the town, and finally return it to the river—unused. There are hundreds of hectares of rich, irrigable land there, enough land to render Msinga agriculturally self-sufficient if it were farmed intensively. But much of it isn't farmed at all. It has lain fallow almost constantly since 1928, its ownership a matter of dispute between sub-tribes of the Zulu nation. A Thembu who sinks a ploughshare into that plain will surely be killed by the Mabaso, and vice versa.

Even the kwaZulu government, a neutral party, cannot use this land. A few years ago, the government assumed direct control of part of the irrigation scheme and invited tribesmen to farm it under government supervision. An official involved in the project was assassinated. After that, kwaZulu formed a cash-crop consortium with some white farmers and planted strawberries on the disputed land. When the first crop was ripe, someone opened the gates and drove hundreds of cattle and donkeys into the strawberry fields. The consortium disintegrated. The government gave up. The land lay fallow and the people of Msinga stayed hungry.

So the Thembu and Mabaso are hostile towards one another,

but that is only the first order of battle in Msinga. The Zulu nation consists of 250 such sub-tribes, seven of which call Msinga home. Those seven sub-tribes are in turn divided into dozens of sub-groups called *isigodi*, each 3,000 to 5,000 strong. An *isigodi* is a neighbourhood, for lack of a better word. This hill is Mashunka, the valley beyond Ngubo. The land to this side of that dry watercourse is Ndlela; the land beyond is Mhlangaan. It takes a Msinga man to know the borders between these *isigodi*, and the consequences that await if he crosses them in wartime. There is nothing to distinguish the people on one side from those on the other. They speak the same language, belong to the same nation, suffer the same deprivations. And yet, every now and then, they fight bloody wars against one another.

Why? It's hard to say. There are several theories, but in the end I preferred the word of an old white policeman who said he didn't really know.

Warrant-Officer Jurgen Freese was a crusty old militarist who lived in a firearm-squad camp on the outskirts of Tugela Ferry. His superiors posted him to Msinga in 1956 and he'd been there ever since. In 1956, there were few roads in Msinga and police still patrolled the valley on horseback. The district was administered by old Africa hands, portly colonials with handlebar moustaches, pith helmets and hides blackened by decades in the sun. The whites played tennis on an old clay court, swam in a pool and sipped pink gins at sunset on the verandas of quaint colonial bungalows. Tugela Ferry was a lost outpost of the dying British Empire.

Jurgen Freese's mission in Msinga was to stamp out the gun trade and combat 'faction fighting', the official term for Msinga's fratricidal wars. In the 1950s, Msinga's wars were honourable, manly affairs, fought under the sun on open plains by half-naked warriors. The death toll was light, and the whole thing was over quickly, usually in a single day. If a man fell in battle, every warrior in the opposing *impi* would stab a blade into his corpse, a traditional Zulu battle ritual.

Such killings were not regarded as murder by the white authorities. They were treated as tribal offences and tried under African law. Whenever someone died in a faction fight, Freese would mount his horse and visit the chief in whose territory the killing had taken place. He would say: 'Listen, you fellows know you're not supposed to do this. Now I want the names of those involved.' The chief and his headmen would confer with the warring parties. Some warriors were appointed to be the accused, others to give evidence. Such decisions were based less on guilt than on a man's ability to pay a fine. On the appointed day, all the warriors would appear before the white magistrate in the court-house at Tugela Ferry. Everyone understood that the trial was essentially a farce, a ritual designed to preserve the white man's face and honour. The witnesses told a yarn, the accused tried to look contrite, the magistrate handed down a few two-pound fines and it was all over.

In the early days, Freese's firearm squad seized the occasional sidearm or hunting rifle, but Msinga's wars were mostly fought with spears and home-made blunderbusses crafted from spare parts and plumbing supplies. As Msinga's migrant labourers were integrated into the white cash economy, however, more and more guns started coming into the district. Battles fought with guns fell outside the legal definition of faction fighting, so warriors who took part in them were charged with murder and tried under white law. 'I suppose the change was well meant,' said Freese, 'but I don't know that it was a good thing.' Once white law started superseding traditional Zulu law, there was virtually no law in Msinga at all.

Msinga's warriors saw little wrong in these killings, you see. They saw no reason why a man who slew an enemy in honourable battle should be taken away and hanged by the white man, so they stopped co-operating with the police. It became hard to find witnesses. Freese's cosy arrangement with the chiefs gave way to elaborate trials in white courts, where white judges followed white evidentiary rules and white lawyers found it easy to confuse and discredit illiterate witnesses. The state case inevitably fell apart in a welter of contradictions and the accused went unpunished in those rare cases where they were charged at all.

It was hard to say how many murderers there were in Msinga, or how many victims they had claimed, because nobody was really counting. Suffice to say Msinga's murder rate was ten to twenty times higher than New York's and its conviction rate so low that it was impossible to measure. It was once the practice to post photographs of executed killers on the wall of Tugela Ferry's court-house. To the best of anyone's recollection, the last time this happened was in 1964.

In the seventies, Msinga's warfare underwent a further evolution, driven this time by soaring sales of the district's chief cash crop, marijuana. Msinga suddenly had money with which to cut big deals on the underground arms market. It was illegal for South African blacks to own guns, but Msinga scoffed at the white man's laws. The latest South African automatic rifles were going into use in Msinga before the South African Defence Force got to test them in combat in Angola. Soviet AK-47s smuggled into the country by brave revolutionaries were sold for beer money on the black market and wound up in the hands of rival factions in the hills above Tugela Ferry.

Msinga's armies dressed to kill in army-surplus combat fatigues and carried deadly modern weaponry, but their campaigns remained curiously archaic. Leaders sought strategic advantage in witchcraft and most soldiers' marksmanship was erratic. They were reluctant to squint down the sights of a rifle in the heat of battle, believing that the spirit of a warrior who died with closed eyes was likely to remain trapped inside his body. So they shot from the hip instead. In 1978, the Sithole hired a white mercenary sharpshooter to aid them in a war against the Zwane and a great slaughter ensued. The sharpshooter decimated the front ranks of the Zwane army, which broke and ran. At day's end, there were fifty-six bodies strewn across the plain. Such battles were rare, though. Msinga's wars were mostly furtive hit-and-run affairs. Combatants were ambushed on lonely footpaths, shot in their huts at night, pulled off buses at road-blocks and executed. Wars that were once over in a day now dragged on for months or even years, unreported even in the South African press. There was always fighting in Msinga, and always had been. In 1978, black officials of the kwaZulu government took over the district's administration and most whites left Tugela Ferry. The tennis-court disappeared under weeds and the swimming-pool was filled with rubble. Only Jurgen Freese stayed on, alone in his Quonset hut on the river bank, with flies buzzing around his head and sweat trickling down his back. His job was impossible. For every gun his squad seized, another came in and there were more corpses to account for. In the end, Msinga turned the man into a Graham Greene character. There was a time when he spent most of his day on his back in his hut, contemplating hell through the bottom of a brandy bottle.

After twenty-seven years in purgatory, Freese retired to the suburbs and quit drinking. Msinga was an intoxicant in its own right, though. He found it hard to readjust to normal life and the South African Police found it equally hard to do without him. And so, when the force asked, Freese returned to Msinga to resume his weary struggle. I found him sitting behind a desk in a prefabricated hut, surrounded by squawking radios and maps festooned with coloured pins and pennants, each marking the site of a trouble-spot. Over a cup of tea, he told me that he had learned a great deal about Msinga in thirty years—enough to know that he knew virtually nothing. 'You will never find out why a war starts,' he said, 'and once it has started, you will never stop it.'

I asked why, and the old policeman shrugged. 'The Zulu is a brave man,' he said. 'You and I would not go into something looking to be killed, but a Zulu will, if honour demands it. To him, death is of no particular concern. An ox is killed; it's eaten. A man gets killed, and his brothers look after his wives and children. That's it. It's no big thing. If we go out to stop a war, the men know we are coming. They watch us with binoculars watching them with binoculars. So we see no guns, but they're there, hidden within a few hundred feet. They are waiting for us to pass. Once we're gone, they collect the guns and start fighting again. We have postponed some wars by arriving, but we've never stopped one. Not ever yet.'

When war was brewing, the police were tipped off by a spy in the dusty post office across the river. The spy knew trouble was coming when women started drifting in to send telegrams to their husbands, fathers and brothers in the cities. All the telegrams contained a similar message: 'There has been a death in the family. Come home.'

Those who did not answer this veiled call to arms were expected to make cash contributions to their faction's war effort, but most men came home. You could not avoid war by staying in Soweto, Kimberley or Pretoria. Disputes rooted in Msinga's dusty hills often bore bloody blossoms in distant white cities. In 1983 in Soweto, one such battle claimed forty-two lives, but slaughter on that scale was unique. Msinga men were more often hunted down singly by hit squads from a rival *isigodi* and killed quietly in their migrant-worker barracks. There was no escape.

So most men came home, dug up their guns, slung greatcoats over their shoulders and headed for the hills, where they lived for the duration. They slept in the open, in the high ravines, plagued by ticks and heat in summer, freezing cold in winter. There was no respite. The war dragged on until enough blood had been shed to satisfy honour. Then the dead were buried but never forgotten. In two years, or five, or ten, the war would flare up again.

That's Msinga; that's the way it is. If you asked Msinga's warriors why they fight, they say that someone stabbed someone else's father at a beer-drink in Kimberley in 1965 and that the insult must be avenged. White academics, on the other hand, advance a theory that revolves around apartheid-induced land hunger and frustration. In Msinga, life is an appallingly grim business. Most people are hungry most of the time. There are no pipes, so women have to carry water on their heads from distant springs and streams. Even firewood is a luxury. In 1975, there was only one school in Msinga and one high-school graduate. Eighty-three per cent of the populace was illiterate. Msinga's population density is 101 per square kilometre, versus fourteen per square kilometre in white South Africa. About eighty per cent of Msinga's people have too little land from which to feed themselves.

It makes complete sense that anyone trapped in such a shithole should want to take up arms and fight. All that's odd about Msinga's wars is that Zulus kill one another, instead of joining forces and wiping out the whites across the border.

4

Oom Flip de Bruin—Uncle Flip—is a great big boulder of a man with a bull neck and prehensile arms that bow out from his muscular body. His face is red from the sun and his hair is thinning now that he's in his fifties. He has a sly smile and chuckle, and a way of looking at you from under his eyelashes that is almost coy, almost shy, almost feline. He is a big sly cat of a man, light on his feet, fast-thinking and probably dangerous—the sort of man to whom violence might come easily and naturally, without passion or anger. On the day I visited, he was wearing shoes but no socks and a plaid shirt hanging out over faded denims. He looked like a huge, overgrown Boer teenager. He told me that he had once been a champion wrestler. 'I have terrible power in my body,' he said. I believed him.

De Bruin was born on a cattle farm in the far western Transvaal on the rim of the Kalahari Desert. He wanted to be a farmer himself, but he was a younger son in a poor white family, so he never got the chance. He quit school after the eighth grade and spent most of his adult life working in a factory. He was a Boer at heart, though, so he always owned a little patch of land somewhere and kept a few cattle on it. When blacks were cleared off Msinga's labour farms and the land put on the market dirt cheap, he saw a chance he'd waited his whole life for. So he bought himself a big chunk of it and became a full-time farmer.

Oom Flip's new farm was an old labour farm. The Zulus driven off it in 1969 were now living in huts and shanties on the far bank of the river, simmering in resentment. They did not exactly welcome their new Boer neighbour. In Msinga, it is said that 'the only law that counts is the law inside a man's head.' In Zulu heads, Flip de Bruin and other whites had taken possession of Zulu land. There were periods of peace along the boundary, but whenever the rains failed, old antagonisms rose to the surface. The Zulus cut white farmers' fences, rustled their stock, stole their crops, hamstrung their cattle and set fire to their grazing land. Along that frontier, most Zulus obeyed one law, the law inside their heads, and most white farmers lived according to another—the law they wrote with their guns.

De Bruin was one of the district's best-known authors of gun legislation. In just one year, ninety-five of his cattle were butchered or stolen, so the Boer retaliated in kind, developing some novel methods of interrogating suspected rustlers and a trigger-happy reputation. He once called to welcome a newcomer to the district and asked, just by way of small talk, how many blacks the stranger had shot in his time. 'None,' said the newcomer. 'I don't believe it,' said Flip de Bruin. 'You've been a farmer all your life, and you've never shot a black?' He was never convicted of murder, so it must have been a joke.

Still, the Zulus had reason to hold all manner of grudges against him. One day, he came home to find his watch-dogs shot dead and his house on fire. In retaliation, de Bruin and his son burned down the nearest Zulu settlement. A week or two later, a party of Zulu gunmen ambushed de Bruin on a lonely road and tried to kill him. He survived only because he was armed himself and ready to return their fire. Flip de Bruin seldom left home without a rifle slung over his shoulder.

'To live here,' he told me, 'you must be strong and positive. You must be direct. You can't walk in two directions. You must be straight and strong and hold true to one line. If you're weak you won't last long here.'

I was about to ask his definition of strength when an illustration of sorts unfolded before my disbelieving eyes. A muscular young white man in a sleeveless T-shirt came running into the farmhouse in a state of agitation. This was Oom Flip's nephew. '*Hulle's daar*,' he shouted—'They're there! They're there!' The boy ran to a padlocked gun-rack and started rattling it frantically. Oom Flip shot out of his armchair, strode to the kitchen door, shielded his eyes and peered into the distance, like a pioneer rancher in a hokey Western, scanning the skyline for hostile Injuns. He shrugged. He and the boy disappeared into a bedroom for a whispered conversation. The boy came out looking crestfallen and walked away. Oom Flip sat down to continue our conversation. I asked what was going on. 'Ag,' he said, 'the boy's crazy.' He offered no further explanation. He just smiled coyly and grinned like a Cheshire cat.

On the far side of the district, I met a man named Roy Cuff, who had once farmed along Msinga's land boundary. While his wife served tea, Mr Cuff sat back to spin some yarns about life on the frontier. Once, he said, he allowed some Zulus displaced by a war to take refuge on his farm. The refugees' enemies concluded that Cuff had formed an alliance against them and he was warned to be ready for an attack. Next thing he knew, his house was full of white cops with machine-guns, ordering him to send his wife away, sleep on the floor and stay away from windows in case an assassin was lurking out there with a high-powered rifle. The attack never materialized. After a few weeks, the war died down and life returned to normal.

In Msinga, normal was like this: you were white and more or less comfortable; the people on the far side of the fence or river were black and desperate. From time to time, they stole a few of your cattle or simply killed one, butchering it on the spot and dragging the bloody haunches back into Msinga. There was no point in calling the police. The people of Msinga didn't assist police inquiries. One of them might, however, sidle up to a white farmer and whisper that so-and-so had been selling fresh meat lately.

Such leads could not be passed on to the police. 'If that man talks to the police,' Cuff explained, 'it's tickets for him. He'll be dead within days.' So there was still no point in calling the police. Instead, said Mr Cuff, 'You get your friends and go to the suspect's kraal at two in the morning. You give him a little experience, so he remembers it was your cow he ate.' I asked what an experience was, but Cuff just shrugged. 'It's an ugly way to live,' he said. 'Both my sons have grown up violent and full of hate. I'm sorry about that.'

Cuff's former next-door neighbour, Peter Gill, was a graduate of one of South Africa's better private schools. He went off into the wilds of Angola and hewed a farm out of virgin bush. When the Angolan civil war broke out in 1975, Gill was caught in the cross-fire. He left Angola with nothing, walking south by night until he ran into the South African army on the Namibian border. After that, he settled in Ian Smith's Rhodesia, where he bought a cut-rate farm in the war zone. He held on to it until Robert Mugabe's guerrillas blasted him out of his fortified farmhouse with rocket-propelled grenades. He returned to South Africa completely penniless and worked on a construction site until he'd saved enough money to buy a half-share in a farm on the Msinga border. The first time he drove on to his new land, someone took a shot at him from behind a bush. OK, he thought, if that's the way they want it, we'll see who wins.

Most of the whites along that border were blind racists, but Gill was a cool-headed man with a clear understanding of the brutal equation into which he was stepping. He arrived in Msinga at the start of a long and merciless drought. The Zulus had been grazing and watering their cattle on his land, so his arrival threatened their survival. Gill didn't contest that or advance spurious moral and legal arguments to justify his actions. He knew that the Zulus were desperate but he was desperate, too. He was rich in Zulu terms but in others he was a poor white. His house would have blended into the hollows of Appalachia and he had no running water. He lost a baby daughter in a very Third Worldly accident; she drowned in an oil drum of trucked-in drinking water. He understood that the Zulus were suffering but saw no room for compromise. As far as Gill was concerned, this had nothing to do with racism. 'I like blacks,' he insisted. He just didn't have enough water or grazing land to share with them. So he took up his gun and secured his boundary.

Any black who set foot on Peter Gill's land was looking for trouble. Even small children stealing water or firewood were likely to find bullets kicking up dust at their feet. Gill had picked up some special-forces skills in the various wars he'd lived through. At night, he blackened his face, donned dark clothing and patrolled his perimeters on foot. 'Basically,' he said, 'I would say that I defended my land as best I could. I used whatever force was necessary.'

Peter Gill was tough. In Msinga, tough was like this: Gill once hired a white farmhand who packed a pistol as he went about his duties. One day, the hired hand strayed a little too close to the Msinga boundary. Some Zulus knocked him out, disarmed him, put the weapon to his head and pulled the trigger. The gun was on safety, though, so the hired hand lived to tell the tale. As soon as the hired hand regained consciousness, however, Gill fired him. 'He was weak,' Gill told me. 'The mere fact that he'd allowed them to flatten his head would have invited more attacks. I was declaring to the Zulus that he wasn't a worthy soldier.

'There's no second prize,' Gill concluded. 'I'm the fastest gun, and while that lasts I'll survive here. The guy with the bigger stick runs things.'

Ask Peter Gill where he lives and he will say Weenen, which means the Place of Weeping in Dutch. Weenen is the white magisterial district that borders black Msinga and it was named in remembrance of the 530 Voortrekkers massacred nearby by the Zulus in 1838. If you pose the same question to the Zulus on the far side of the boundary fence, however, they will say that Gill lives in Nobamba, the Place Where We Caught The Whites. What hope of reconciliation is there in such a place? I saw none. That river was just another front in the war without end—the war that started in the 1780s along the Great Fish River and continues to this day. Nothing has been forgiven, nothing forgotten, nothing settled.

5

Into this vortex of hatred and violence, in the winter of 1975, stepped Neil and Creina Alcock. Theirs was the last farm in white South Africa, separated from Msinga in the west by a rusting fence, in the south by the Tugela River. Their land began by the river, climbed over a line of hills and stretched away across the vast plain beyond. On the day they arrived, Neil and Creina walked the eroded hills, strewing handfuls of wild-grass seed into the wounds of the ruined land. They decided to name the new farm Mdukatshani, the Place of Lost Grasses, but they were already dreaming of another Msinga, a place where grass grew tall and green.

Neil and Creina once set their vision down in a document entitled *Msinga 2000*, less a blueprint for development than a dream of how Msinga might one day be. In the dream, furrows led spring water down Msinga's barren hillsides and into tiny gardens, where Zulu kraal-holders reaped vegetables in soils enriched by manure and the phosphate-rich ashes of cattle bones. Each Zulu kraal was shaded by fruit trees and surrounded by beehives. Each had its own fish-pond and poultry run, its own solar cooker and gas-digester— a digester being a low-tech oil-drum contraption designed to transform dung into methane gas. In the dream, this gas replaced wood as Msinga's fuel, allowing the last trees to be spared in order to stabilize the eroding slopes. On the hillsides, the dongas had been blocked with stone packs and they were slowly silting up. Now that the cattle were communally herded and grazed in rotating camps, grass was returning to the wasteland and all the cattle were fat again.

The people of this fortunate valley drew their wisdom from Mdukatshani. In the dream, there was a school for children at Mdukatshani and a 'barefoot university' where their fathers studied farming and conservation. Mdukatshani also had a plant nursery, a veterinary clinic and a cattle stud with prime bulls for injecting good blood into Msinga's scrawny herd. As the dream drew to a close, Msinga's gardens were blooming, its milk-pails overflowing, its people plump and healthy. A near-desert had been transformed into Eden and it had all been accomplished without purchased fertilizer or chemicals, tractors or gasoline. Msinga couldn't afford such things. If it were to survive and feed itself, it had to do so with existing resources: sun, water, the dung of animals and the sweat of men. 'For the Msingas of Africa,' Neil concluded, 'and there are many, there is no other way.'

Neil's was a new way, a new approach to the problems of a continent where other ways had already failed. It was clear, by 1975, that Africa was heading towards a state of permanent famine. Well-intentioned Westerners were trying to help, but grafts of alien agricultural technology just didn't seem to take in Africa. Development workers would move into the continent's dustbowls with heads full of university theory and pockets bulging with UN or EEC or USAID cash. They'd construct huge dams, plough up plains, install batteries of diesel pumps and centre-pin irrigation systems. And then they'd go home and things would fall apart. Machines broke down and stayed broken down. Few Africans had the skills to maintain complex equipment and there were no spare parts anyway. Within a year or two, the peasants had returned to scuffling the dust with hoes and donkey ploughs, and there was little left to see for the new missionaries' efforts save the rusting hulks of imported machinery and futile scratches on the face of the land.

This was often cited, in South Africa and elsewhere, as proof of African incompetence. In Neil Alcock's judgement, it was more likely proof of Western arrogance. It was axiomatic that African peasants were too backward to make plans for themselves, so the new missionaries did it for them. Then they set off for the wastelands in air-conditioned caravans and tried to impose their nostrums on people who had little idea of what they were talking about.

Neil, on the other hand, was something of a peasant himself, a white farmer with a tenth-grade education. He believed in African farmers and thought they were quite wise enough to devise solutions to their own problems. Such solutions, moreover, were the only ones that would work—African solutions, using African methods and African technologies. As Neil saw it, the role of a Western man, an educated man, was to place himself and his skills at the disposal of the peasantry—to stop dictating and start advising. He also thought some patience was called for. A two-year tour of duty in some famine-stricken African hell hole clearly helped no one. As far as Neil Alcock was concerned, you had to live among Africans, like an African, until you saw through African eyes, until African problems became your own problems and African pain became your pain. It didn't matter whether it took years, even decades. To be effective, a white man had to earn the right of trust and acceptance. Only then could he turn to his black brothers and say: 'We are in the dust, my friends; but there is a way out, and I will show it to you.'

Neil was not so naïve as to believe his vision would be easily realized, but he was brave enough to try. A lesser man would have given up on day one. Neil arrived in Msinga with a piece of paper saying that Church Agricultural Projects owned 6,000 acres of land. In Msinga, such paper meant nothing. The only land to which Neil could truly lay claim was the few hundred acres visible from his riverside settlement. The land beyond the hills, away from the river, was not really his and never would be. The Alcocks called it the top country, and it was Zulu country, in terms of the law inside Zulu heads. Zulus cut wood on it, hunted across it, grazed and watered their cattle on it. If anyone controlled the top country, it was the cattle thieves and bandits who lived along its border.

For such men, Neil's arrival was too good to be true. Eight hundred fat cattle and nobody to guard them but a white man with no guns and a handful of tame Zulu Christians from some up-country mission. Neil didn't have enough hands to herd the cattle, let alone guard them against human predators. They were easy game. One by one and then by the dozen, the cattle started disappearing, driven off in the night down the Skhelenge Gorge, across the river and into the wild heart of Msinga. The police did nothing but take statements, so Neil and his henchmen tracked down some stolen cattle on their own and provided the police with evidence for a few convictions. If anything, this worsened the rustling and drew threats of retribution. The mission Zulus were terrified. One by one, they deserted and returned to safer climes. In just two months, seventy of the project's cattle were stolen; almost half as many again died of heartwater, a low-veld cattle disease. 'We were hanging on,' said Creina, 'by the tips of our fingers, on the brink of utter disaster.'

And so Neil's dream of continuing the cattle co-operative and ultimately extending it into Msinga came to nothing. It became clear that as long as the project ran cattle, the Zulu would regard Neil as a competitor, not a friend, and he'd have to hold them off with guns, like his white neighbours. Rather than turn Mdukatshani into an armed encampment, the project's directors decided to sell the communal cattle herd and reach an understanding with the people of Msinga. They would henceforth be welcome to graze cattle and collect firewood on the project's land, provided that they co-operated with Neil's conservation schemes. It was an eminently fair deal and it brought a measure of peace to Mdukatshani's sector of the frontier.

Once the cattle were gone, Neil turned his attention to agricultural development, to the vision contained in the *Msinga 2000* document. He invited Msinga men to a series of *indaba*s, or open-air meetings, where he laid out his plans. The Zulus were too polite to say so, but they thought this white man was mad. He claimed it was possible to grow food in the dust in waterless places without spending any money. Even a child knew that was nonsense.

So Neil and some helpers set out to prove them wrong. They purloined some railway tracks from an abandoned siding and built a towering scaffold on the river bank. Then they took a tractor tyre, cut it into scoop-like segments and bolted it spokewise on to the hub of an old tractor wheel. A system of pulleys lowered the wheel into the river. The rubber scoops dipped into the swift brown torrent and spun the tractor hub, which turned the differential from a scrapped Land Rover, which drove a pump, which delivered water to a dry, stony garden site hundreds of yards away. There, in soil fertilized by dung and the ash of cattle bones, some Zulu women planted and reaped a bumper crop of vegetables. Surrounding communities were hugely impressed. Beyond that point, the scheme started moving forward.

Neil organized a committee of tribal elders to run the project, casting himself as their humble servant and technical advisor. The committee was nominally in charge, but it was Neil who really made things happen. He was a man who could stand on a barren, eroded hillside, miles from the nearest water, surrounded by incredulous peasants, and say: 'There will be a dam here.' And a lo, a dam there would be, or a weir across the river, or an irrigation furrow to carry a trickle of precious water from a distant spring to tiny patches of tillable land. Bankrolled by donations from churches, foreign governments and the Anglo-American conglomerate, he hired armies of Zulus and set them to work on a vast Iron Age engineering project—laying furrows, stringing fences, blocking dongas with dikes of stone. Dams were dug with shovels, the dirt carried off in buckets on women's heads. Neil drew plans in the dust with sticks and judged levels with his naked eye. If a boulder lay in the path of one of his furrows, Zulu women built a bonfire under it, heated it until it glowed, then doused it with pails of water. *Voilá.* The rock shattered. Zulu dynamite, they called it.

In the spring of 1977, the first water came trickling down the furrows and into the pioneer gardens and, for a while, the dream seemed to be coming true. In her monthly newsletter to donors and supporters, Creina wrote: 'We sense the beginnings of a small revolution.' Mdukatshani became a place of pilgrimage for young white volunteers yearning to atone for the sins of their fathers. A steady stream of foreign diplomats and new missionaries came to see the project for themselves.

The man who met visitors at the project's gates was getting on towards sixty now, completely grey and balding. Neil was always wearing dusty jeans and car-tyre sandals, and the first thing he showed off was always his water-wheel; he was immensely proud of his water-wheel. After that, visitors were escorted through a complex of eleven houses, huts and workshops, all built in the Zulu fashion of mud, stone and thatch and costing less than 125 dollars apiece. In the workshops, Zulus were assembling experimental solar cookers and beating old oil drums into prototypical methane digesters. There was a fish-pond stocked with bass and *tilapia*, and an earthen cave full of glowing glass beads, the raw materials of a thriving craft project. Under Creina's direction, the beads were turned into Zulu jewellery of astonishing beauty and sold in the distant cities.

As visitors did the rounds, they were introduced to tongue-tied black men who turned out to be the leaders of the project. Mdukatshani's dignified chairman, Petros Majozi, was formerly a cook in a Johannesburg hotel. The resident engineer was Mphephete Masondo, who had never seen the inside of a school. A former police constable, the flamboyant Elijah Mhlongo, was chief of security. The general manager, Bokide Khumalo, couldn't read or write, but he gave orders to white volunteers with impressive university degrees.

At some point, you might have seen Neil scribble his daily love letter to his wife and hand it to a herdboy, who scurried off to deliver it. Creina spent her days in a mud 'office' on the cliff-top, bashing away on a portable typewriter on a 'desk' of river stone. She was still editing *African Wildlife* by mail and in her spare time writing reports and newsletters to the project's supporters. At the outset, her newsletters were quite dry and factual, but as she and Neil got to know Msinga better they evolved into literature. Fantastic characters moved across her pages, engaged in utterly improbable undertakings. An ancient Zulu gunsmith sat under a thorn tree in the bush, fashioning scrap-metal shotguns with his bare hands. An illiterate dope-farmer in the high ravines devised an automatic irrigation system that would have earned a Masters in engineering at any Western university. The newsletters were a window into a secret world—the world of rural black South Africans, the country's invisible people. Creina refused to allow them to be published, so they were passed from hand to hand until they fell apart at the staples.

If the visitors were really fortunate, Neil might row them across the river to see the work being done in Msinga itself. They saw irrigation furrows leading water from springs in the hills. They saw the first crops coming up in tiny gardens, fenced against goats with loans from the project's Small Farmer's Trust. They sometimes met ragged black men and women who made solemn statements in broken English. They would declare: 'We are weak, but when Neil is with us we feel strong. We cannot write, but he is teaching us to write with grass on the hillsides.' Or simply: 'God is sending *Numyaan* to help the people.' *Numyaan* is a Zulu honorific meaning squire.

Come sunset, they met the rest of the Alcock household—the white sons, G.G. and Rauri, and the black sons, seven barefoot Zulu herdboys whom the Alcocks had more or less adopted. Mboma, the eldest, had red hair when he first moved in with the Alcocks—a symptom of the nutritional disease kwashiorkor. He soon recovered, though, and blossomed into an artful dodger, an exceptionally bright child who swiftly mastered English and the allied art of manipulating white volunteers. Creina's sister Kathy wrote a children's book about Mboma's life and hard times, which included a spell as a ten-year-old labourer on a white farm in the district. *Story of a Herdboy* became a minor best seller in the world's bookshops. Mboma Dladla's name was even mentioned in the United Nations, in the course of a debate on 'slave labour' in South Africa.

Mboma was G.G.'s best friend. Among Rauri's best friends was a boy named Sensilube, whose parents had been murdered for stealing their neighbour's cattle. The Alcocks caught him milking their cows, discovered his plight and took him in. A third boy was Ndudu, a witty little spiv who dreamed of going to Soweto when he grew up and becoming a fancy bootlegger. The black sons and white sons slept in adjoining huts, ate and played together and explored the surrounding countryside on horseback. In many ways, the white boys were assimilated Zulu. They spoke the Zulu language like Zulus. They knew how to suck sweet jelly from a hole in the stem of an aloe flower, how to set snares for birds and small game. From Mboma, they learned the best game of all—riding the raging river on driftwood after a summer thunderstorm. It was only in their teens, when they went away to high school, that G. G. and Rauri realized how unorthodox their childhood had been.

And finally, of course, there was Creina. She was the last

person you expected to meet in a mud hut. She wore rags and tatters, eschewed make-up and never shaved her legs, but she remained truly beautiful. She could talk knowledgeably about almost anything—literature, science, the arcana of apartheid legislation, the botany of the thorn veld, agricultural production in the Sudan. There you were in a mud hut, with ants in your food and tadpoles in your coffee, making small talk with a ravishing intellectual who graced her wisdoms with quotes from great philosophers and poets. It all seemed highly improbable.

After supper, Neil sank into the depths of his wicker chair and told stories in the firelight. He'd talk about—oh, the history of the tribes in the region, or the inner workings of the local dope trade, or hapless secret policemen he had known. Some of his best yarns concerned his white neighbours, many of whom referred to him as *die groot terroris*—'the master terrorist' supposedly trained in Red China. It was said that he and his wife had 'kaffir' lovers. It was said that Creina stripped naked and washed in the river in full view of any black man who happened to be passing by.

And finally, it was said that the Alcocks were stirring the Zulus to revolt, even arming them. From time to time, the secret police picked up the project's Zulu staff and interrogated them on that score. What did Alcock say? Was he a communist? Why did he live like a kaffir? What was wrong with him? Was he mad? Lots of whites thought he was mad, living the way he did, in a mud hut, eating 'bloody plant soup' or whatever it was that Africans survived on.

Come bedtime, visitors groped their way up a dark footpath and into a mud hut, where they lay under coarse woollen blankets, listening to the river roaring over rapids and staring at the smoke-darkened thatch. Later, many would struggle to describe what they'd experienced that day. They were white and came from a culture that had lost the ability to discuss matters of the heart without diminishing them inside quotes or disarming them with cynical asides. One such visitor was a former Rhodes Scholar who held very high office in a multinational corporation. When I asked him what he made of Neil Alcock, he vacillated, coughed embarrassedly and said: 'One was struck by his non-materialistic attitude.'

Rian Malan

Well, that was certainly true. Mdukatshani was arguably the most cost-efficient development project in Africa. At one point, the project's funding level was 1,250 dollars a month—just about enough to cover the salary of a single United Nations development worker. In Neil Alcock's hands, it kept an entire project running, paying the salaries of sixty-nine black and five white staff members. The Alcocks' cut was about fifty dollars. On that kind of money, you lived in a mud hut, very simply, and were liable to be mistaken for a saint, a missionary, a man of God and all sorts of other things that Neil Alcock wasn't.

He was a complete stranger to sanctimony. He mocked self-righteous solemnity and cracked jokes about bearded liberals behind their backs. He didn't mind living in a mud hut. If anything, he liked it. He liked farming, liked cattle and liked nothing better than sitting under a thorn tree, disputing with Zulu men. There is a Zulu saying, 'I see you with my heart.' Neil saw Zulus that way, and that was the way they saw him.

His arrival in the district, in 1975, had caused fear and consternation on the far side of the boundary fence. Most Zulus had long since ceased to trust whites. When Neil announced that he'd come to help them, they listened impassively, then went home and tried to divine the trick. They spent hours arguing about him, trying to figure out exactly what he was up to and how he intended to rip them off. Word of his arrival filtered back to Johannesburg's migrant-worker hostels and the debates continued there. When someone informed Johan Dladla that a white had arrived in Msinga, talking nonsense about working together and sharing the land, he clicked his tongue angrily. 'Black and white can never work together,' he said.

On his next trip home, Dladla visited the project and told Neil so to his face. 'Black and white can never work together,' he said. Neil just laughed and invited Dladla to sit down for a talk. They saw each other's hearts and Johan Dladla was won over. He never went back to Jo'burg. He resigned his city job and stayed to work with the white man.

Another man who never went back was Petros Majozi, who eventually became the project's chairman. Majozi had always yearned to be a farmer, but that option was closed to a Zulu family

76

man. A Zulu man had to go to the white cities and earn cash so that his family could 'farm at the store'. So Majozi spent thirty-six years in Johannesburg, living in some lonely servants' quarters and longing for his home. He had four children back in Msinga, plus a wife and a small herd of beloved cattle, but he saw them only once a year.

On 9 January 1975, the last day of his annual holiday, Petros Majozi was driving his cattle through the bush, leaden with sadness at the thought of leaving the next day, when a white man materialized before him. Majozi's knees turned to water. He was on no-man's-land—land that belonged to whites on paper but to the Zulus in their heads. He thought the white would surely pull a gun, impound his cattle and maybe arrest him, too. Instead, Neil smiled and said hello in Zulu. They sat down under a tree and talked about land and cattle for a while, and then Neil continued on his way. It was such an insignificant encounter that Neil promptly forgot about it.

Petros Majozi, on the other hand, had seen a white man with his heart. The next morning, he took the bus to Tugela Ferry, joined a queue outside the post office and telephoned his white boss in Johannesburg. 'I'm not coming back,' he said.

Majozi was a highly valuable employee, so the boss demanded to know why.

'I met a white man who will help me to farm,' said Majozi.

'How long have you known him?' asked the boss.

'I have only met him once,' Majozi replied.

'And how much is he paying you?'

'Nothing.'

'Your family will starve,' said the white man.

'I hope not,' said Majozi.

'You will lose your pension,' said the white man.

'I don't care,' Majozi replied. The white man at the other end of the line was at an utter loss to understand how a level-headed and intelligent man could take such a risk on the basis of a chance encounter in the bush, and Majozi was at a loss to explain it. His English was halting and besides, white men knew little about seeing with the heart. So Majozi just said, 'I'm sorry,' and put the telephone down.

And then he took the bus back to Mdukatshani, went to see Neil and told him that he also believed in working together. 'We must take this fright in our hearts,' he said, 'and throw it in the river.'

And so Majozi and many others threw in their lot with Neil and for three years all went well. Mdukatshani became a sort of dusty Camelot, a congenial spot where it was possible to believe, if only for a moment, that South Africa's problems might all be sorted out. It was just a small agricultural project in a forgotten corner of the country, but there was nowhere else quite like it. It lay astride the country's most bitter old frontier, and if love could flourish there it could surely flourish anywhere.

Or so it seemed, at any rate.

6

The road linking Mdukatshani to the village of Weenen is as bad as any other in Msinga. It winds along the river bank, crosses the Bushman's River on a causeway, climbs a rugged hill and heads on across the plain beyond. It is not a good road to drive in convoy. The wheels of the vehicle ahead raise clouds of choking dust and spray stones into your windshield, and if the vehicle ahead is a bus the journey becomes absolutely intolerable. One morning, Creina got stuck behind a lumbering bus on her way into town and ate dust for several miles. It was hard to overtake another vehicle on Msinga's dirt roads. In the end, though, she saw an opening, shot past the bus and travelled on towards Weenen.

It was around Christmas 1978. The Alcocks had been in Msinga for three and a half years and were starting to feel less like strangers. Visitors' first impressions to the contrary, their first years in Msinga hadn't been all that easy. They were struggling to control the project's boundaries. A Zulu headman who had given evidence on their behalf in a goat-theft case had been murdered for his trouble. Indeed, there had been many murders, but that was the nature of Msinga, reflected in its very place names. In Zulu, Tugela Ferry was known as *Mshaya Safa*—Hit Him Till He's Dead. In Msinga, you could get killed for almost anything—for having the wrong name, or the wrong address, or ploughing disputed land. Mdukatshani's black bookkeeper, Anton Hlongwane, was so scared of being murdered that he refused to send out notices to Zulu debtors. Still, the Alcocks had persevered in spite of all problems and imagined they had already seen Msinga's worst side. But they had seen nothing, nothing, nothing.

The bus Creina had just passed, for instance, was about to run into trouble. As it rounded a bend, a platoon of black men armed with rifles stepped into the road and forced the driver to halt. The gunmen boarded the bus, pulled five male passengers off it and executed them. Creina knew nothing of this, of course. She drove on into Weenen, bought supplies and headed back towards the project. En route, she found the road closed by a line of big boulders. The Zulus travelling with her were too scared to move, so Creina asked one of her sons to get out and roll the rocks aside. She had not been in Msinga long enough to know when to be afraid.

A few miles farther on, at the gates of the project, she came upon a harrowing sight—a Zulu truck driver with a bullet in his abdomen, bleeding to death in Neil's arms. The driver had been ambushed at the line of boulders—the sixth man shot on that road in a single morning. What on earth was this? Where were the police? Where on earth was the ambulance? The fatally injured man had been lying in the sun for hours. An ambulance finally came and the Alcocks retired to the rocks above the river, to recover from the traumas of the day.

And then they looked up and saw something amazing: a skirmish line of heavily armed black men in military uniforms, advancing towards them on the river's far bank. The Alcocks had been in Msinga for three years, but this was their first sighting of a Zulu *impi*. Most whites would have fled in terror, but not Neil Alcock. He walked down to the water, cupped his hands and yelled: 'Go away! We don't want you here with guns!' The Zulu warriors stood their ground, though. They had come to escort one of their brothers to safety and wouldn't leave until he had crossed the river to join them. Then they retreated into the hills.

And so ended the first of many bad days in Msinga. There had been wars elsewhere in the district in the preceding three years, but none near Mdukatshani until now. As Neil and Creina understood it, a young man from the Majola faction, a few miles up-river, had tried to seduce the girl-friend of a rival Madondo. Now young men were killing one another in consequence, killing innocent truck drivers, too. In the ensuing three months, the Majola-Madondo war claimed twenty-seven lives. Just as it was dying down, another war broke out across the river, sparked off this time by a disagreement over the outcome of a tribal dancing competition in a Johannesburg migrants' hostel. Members of the losing team refused to abide by the judges' decision. The argument escalated into violence, so the migrants came home, took up their guns and settled the dispute in the hills. That war was no sooner over than a third broke out, triggered this time by the murder of a Zulu headman whose testimony put a cattle-thief behind bars.

The Alcocks were dismayed. At the outset, they'd believed that all Msinga's problems were rooted in land hunger and apartheid and would respond to 'a little social engineering', as Creina put it. Now it dawned on them that it was not going to be quite that easy. From 1979 onwards, Neil and Creina lived amid constant terror. Bands of gunmen roamed the farm and set up ambushes on the roads that crossed it. There were tracers in the sky at night and the ravines resounded with gunfire during the day. The wars made development work very difficult. As soon as the first shot was fired, men disappeared and their wives stopped working, too—they had to carry food and water to their husbands' secret lairs. A war could last months, even years, and while it raged there was little the Alcocks could do save ferry the dead and wounded to the hospital. By the end of 1979, a note of despair was creeping into Creina's newsletters. She closed one with a quote from the poet Roy Campbell: *The hurricanes of chaos have begun to buzz like hornets in the shifting sands.*

The following year, the rains failed and the coffin lid started closing on Neil's dream. The grass withered, crops shrivelled and Zulu cattle started dying by the thousand. On top of the drought came two more wars among the Zulus. After war came pestilence— first cholera, then rabies—and after pestilence came famine. The fish in Neil's pond went belly-up in the foul water. His methane gas-digesters turned out to be impractical and had to be abandoned.

The solar cookers tarnished and were thrown out to rust. White volunteers tired of reading their Marx in mud huts and left to find easier ways of fighting apartheid. The irrigation system at Dimbi was spotted by helicopter-borne narcotics police on a search-and-destroy mission. Taking it for a marijuana farm, they landed and destroyed it. The springs in the hills dried up and the river dwindled to a turgid trickle.

In 1981, the rains failed again. Beyond that point, Neil and Creina's lives seem to assume the quality or a myth or fable; event succeeds event with the random disconnectedness of a dream or nightmare; the plot unfolds according to the caprice of cruel and vengeful gods. The last white volunteer to work on Mdukatshani told me she left because there seemed to be no end to Msinga's crises and no resolution to any of them. They rolled in like breakers on to a beach, one after the other, with no time between to recover. 'Msinga's such a confused and destroyed place,' she said. 'I felt completely blindfolded and helpless. There was nothing you could do except rave at somebody.' So Neil raved. He raved for years, at anyone with the power to help—the Red Cross, white newspapers, relief organizations, even the apartheid government. He raved so long and so loud that there came a time when even his liberal allies could no longer bear to listen. In 1981, he wrote a series of letters to old friends in the liberal movement, asking why they had abandoned him to his 'fatigue, inefficiency and failure'. He asked: 'Why me alone?' No replies came. He was on his own.

The drought dragged on until 1982, only to break in a raging cloudburst. The canal at Mseleni was buried by a landslide, the dam at Umhlumba washed away by a flood. The river came down in spate and crippled Neil's beloved water-wheel. After that single thunderstorm, the skies cleared and the sun beat down more mercilessly than ever.

By September 1982, it was clear that Neil Alcock had met his match in Msinga. After three rainless years, there was little to show for his efforts save some bone-dry furrows, empty dams, a weir across the river and a single garden in which the two widows of one Philemon Khoza were growing enough vegetables to feed themselves. 'Those two women,' he said in a heart-breaking report to donors, 'must serve as our example of what can be achieved.' Otherwise, it was all dust to dust and chaos to chaos.

I s this beginning to sound like hell to you? It sounded that way to me when I first heard it, and yet it was really a love story, a story about two whites who loved Africa. Love drew Neil and Creina to Msinga and love kept them there, in their mud hut in the dust, even though staying meant Neil's death. He had leukaemia, you see, and he was dying. He'd been advised that he had five years to live and that if he wanted all of them, he had to eat fresh meat, milk and cheese. There was no electricity on Mdukatshani and hence no refrigerator. In Msinga's torrid summers, milk curdled in minutes, meat rotted within a day. If Neil wanted to live, he had to leave. He had made a commitment to stay for ever, though, and he kept it.

Towards the end, Neil and Creina's life became what life must be for the overwhelming majority of people on this sad continent. They lived from day to day, season to season, with little hope of salvation and no certainties save the certainty of death. Those mute, starving people we see on TV, cradling their dying children in their arms—is that not how life is for them? How else do they see it, if not that way? And yet, to hear Creina tell it, it was often a life of unbearable ecstasy. She did not dwell on the despair and defeat. Instead, she spoke of the hot dust between her toes and the water of the river cool against her skin. She spoke of men who greeted trees as they walked through the bush and children who ducked away from the face in the glass because they had never seen themselves in a mirror. She spoke of the nobility and courage of Zulu warriors and the strength of their widows. She spoke of Christmas Eve, when the migrants came home from the cities and the valley rang with the sound of bugles and hooters and the joyful cries of children who had not seen their fathers for a full year.

And she told me about the time their hut burned down. She and Neil lost what little they had in that fire. As word of their misfortune spread, Zulus started converging on Mdukatshani from miles around. Some were old, some were total strangers and all were desperately poor, and yet they came to help the white man. Some offered gifts of cash and those who had nothing offered their muscles, to help with the rebuilding. One ancient man tried to press a tattered banknote into Neil's hand. He must have been hoarding it for decades and now he was offering it to a white man.

Afterwards, if anyone asked Neil why he stayed even though it meant dying, he mentioned that day—the day the poorest black people dug up their buried treasure and offered it to him. He and Creina had yearned all their lives to belong in Africa and it seemed that Africa had finally accepted them and returned their embrace. After that, he could not forsake his people, and so he stayed and Creina stayed with him.

Towards the end of 1982, Neil's end seemed near. His body lost the ability to heal itself. The smallest scratch festered and soon his face and legs were covered with suppurating sores. He ran a constant fever and his skin was hot to the touch. He lay down in the windless heat on the flat rocks beside the dwindling river and made ready to die. He didn't die, though; he was too tough. He somehow pulled through. He was too weak to walk, so he had a horse brought to the door and, on its back, he mounted his last crusade.

7

It was a hot summer afternoon and the herdboys were watching the sky. There were three of them, all Zulu teenagers, guarding their fathers' cattle on the plain of Ngongolo on the far side of Mdukatshani's hills. Thunder-clouds were building above them and the boys were worried about lightning. They didn't want to be caught in the open by an electrical storm. And so, when the sky darkened and started spitting, they abandoned their duties and ran home to sit out the storm. After a while, the rain stopped and the sun came out again. The trio of herdboys ventured out on to the rain-swept plain, only to find that their cattle had scattered in the storm. The spoor ran through a hole in the boundary fence and into white South Africa—into land that belonged to 'the soldier'.

The soldier's real name was James Christie, but the Zulus didn't know that. When he first bought land on the border, Zulus asked who he was, but Christie wouldn't say. 'I come from the world,' he said. Then he flipped an eyelid and displayed the white of an eye—a gesture of insult and malevolent intent. In the year or two since, James Christie had become a figure of dread for the Zulus on the far side of the fence. He didn't farm the land himself but he came by from time to time to make sure that the Zulus weren't grazing their stock on it in his absence. On these patrols, he wore combat fatigues, carried a gun and usually shot any Zulu goats or cattle he came across on his side of the fence. The Africans alleged that he also fired warning shots at them and, in one instance, broke the jaw of a man caught trespassing on his land. The herdboys knew all this but they had no choice—they had to cross the boundary to retrieve their cattle.

They were not many paces inside white South Africa when the soldier stepped out from behind some bushes with a shotgun in his hands. '*Ja, madoda*,' he said in Zulu, 'what are you doing on my land?' And then he pulled the trigger. The boys fled, one limping on a leg full of buckshot, another with a wound in his back. Only when they were safely back in Msinga did the second boy collapse, 'breathing bubbles through a hole in his back.'

The wounded teenager was rushed to a hospital in Pietermaritzburg, where surgeons operated to remove shot lodged close to his heart. A week or two later, when the boy was well enough to walk again, his father and some relatives took him to the police station in Weenen to press charges against the white gunman. The policeman behind the desk was white. 'Is it true,' he asked the boy, 'that you were walking on a white man's land at the time of the shooting?'

'Yes,' the boy replied.

'Well,' said the policeman, 'if I had been that farmer, I would have put the bullet here.' He leaned over the desk and put a finger against the black youngster's temple, and that was just about the end of that as far as law enforcement was concerned. The shooting was just another skirmish in a very old war—the war of blacks and whites over land.

Men on both sides of the Msinga border kept cattle and there was too little land to go round, especially for men who were black. The average Msinga cattleman had access to about nine hectares of tribal land. His counterpart in white South Africa owned 598. These were the basic, brutal facts of life along the border and all else flowed from them. If it rained, the border remained more or less peaceful; if it didn't, there was trouble. In times of drought, Msinga's grazing was swiftly depleted and starving Zulu livestock started piling up along the boundary fence, staring dumbly into white South Africa, where some grass and water remained. For a Zulu, a cow was no mere beast of utility. Each cow had a name and was spoken to as though she were a member of the family. When a starving cow sank to her knees in the dust and couldn't get up again, her owner sank down and cried alongside her. Rather than see their cattle die, the Zulus started cutting fences and turning them loose on white land. Whites responded with their guns and the border became a virtual free-fire zone.

Some white farmers simply shot Zulu goats and cattle, but others found a way to profit from the war. They rounded up trespassing livestock and drove it to the government pound. The Zulus had to pay stiff fines for the release of their animals and most of the money went straight into the white farmer's pocket as compensation for damage to his land. Zulus charged that some whites were actually luring Zulu cattle on to their land with a view to exacting fines. They also alleged that they were routinely assaulted or shot at for trespassing on white land, but the police turned a blind eye to such complaints. Indeed, there came a time when the Zulus no longer bothered to report these matters to the police. They seldom took action against white men. In the case of the herdboys shot by James Christie, for instance, the police took some statements and a photograph of the scene of the shooting, but nothing happened after that. More than two years passed but no charges were filed.

One day, however, a messenger of court showed up at James Christie's place and handed him an official-looking envelope. Christie ripped it open and snorted with indignation. The herdboys were suing him in civil court for assault and attempted murder. A while later, Flip de Bruin received a similar communication. In his case, the plaintiff was a suspected Zulu cattle-thief who had allegedly been subjected to one of de Bruin's novel interrogations—made to crawl through the veld on all fours for half a mile while the Boer prodded him onward with a spear. Soon after that, Peter Gill started receiving visits from detectives asking questions about his habit of using force to defend his land. Neil Alcock's last crusade was under way.

Neil had two allies in this campaign—the Legal Resources Centre, a Durban-based legal services foundation, and a Zulu matron with a seventh-grade education. Mrs Nattie Duma was almost as round as she was tall and her heart was as big as the rest of her. She was Neil's private eye. Whenever a white man raised his fists or gun to a black man, Nattie Duma came sniffing around on his farm, conducting surreptitious interviews with the injured parties. She gave the details to Neil, who passed them on to the Legal Resources Centre and encouraged them to sue the bastard.

In all, Neil and Nattie investigated some forty allegations of assault and wrongdoing by local whites in the final years of his life. One case involved an eighty-six-year-old black man who was allegedly kicked, beaten and dragged around by the nose by a white farmer. Another involved a farm labourer who made the mistake of asking his *baas* for his wages. He was beaten up, loaded in a car, dumped in the veld, collected again and taken to the police, who charged him with trespassing. A third case involved a Zulu woman who claimed she'd been raped by a white farmer and produced a half-breed twelve-year-old daughter to prove it. The white man, Phil Opperman of the farm Darkest Africa, denied all knowledge of the incident. A blood test proved he was lying, though, and he was ordered to start paying child support.

That story made headlines throughout the country and didn't draw Neil Alcock any closer to the hearts of local whites. The lawsuit that finally outraged them, however, was the so-called roads dispute. In the roads dispute, Neil's stated aim was to force the reopening of certain traditional rights of way, thus restoring to Zulus the right to travel cross-country from Msinga to Weenen or down to the river. As far as his white neighbours were concerned, it was something else entirely. The disputed rights of way ran across white-owned land; if they were reopened, Zulus would be legally entitled to drive their cattle on to white farms and water them at any point where the path crossed a watercourse. In white minds, the lawsuit raised the spectre of huge herds of starving Zulu goats and cattle trekking back and forth between Msinga and their dwindling dams, devouring their last grazing *en route*. The whites were appalled. They thought Neil was trying to drive them off their land. They were probably right.

White farmers weren't the only target of Neil's final campaign. 'Towards the end,' a government official told me, 'he made life impossible for everyone.' He sued the Tugela Ferry police for torturing suspects. He raised a hue and cry about police corruption. He had embarrassing questions asked in parliament and twisted the government's arm until it set up a commission to arbitrate Weenen-Msinga border tensions. In the process, he made himself the most hated white man in central Natal. His telephone rang at odd hours and anonymous Boer voices warned him that his time was coming. The local branch of the ruling National Party passed a resolution imploring the government to remove Alcock from their midst. The secret police sent out a detachment to investigate charges of 'racial incitement'. Neil didn't flinch. If anything, he fought harder as his allotted five years ran out.

In 1983, the rains failed yet again and the screws on Msinga tightened. Zulu cattle were dying again but the disputed rights of way remained closed. There was no time to wait for justice to run its course, so Neil took matters into his own hands. He and his sons and brother went out one night with picks and axe-handles and forced one of the disputed roads open. They broke chains, smashed padlocks, tore the gates off their hinges and threw them into the nearest gulley. Then they dumped the broken chains and padlocks on a white farmer's doorstep, as if daring him to do something. In rural South Africa, such behaviour was virtually suicidal. Neil Alcock was looking for trouble and there came a time when he seemed likely to get it soon.

Some five miles up-river from Mdukatshani there lived a white man named Tom Uren, a British citizen who'd spent many years in Kenya. He'd recently arrived in Msinga to manage a farm called Sun Valley. Whites regarded Uren as a sound fellow, a good, strict farm manager, but blacks were reputed to hate him, claiming that he docked their wages for infringements of arbitrary rules and put the money into his own pocket. One day, Uren got out of his pick-up to open a gate on a lonely road. A shot rang out and he fell dead with a bullet in his head. Some whites immediately blamed Neil Alcock. 'Figure it out for yourself,' one told me. 'He wanted the kaffirs to have our land, so we had to be chased away. He was encouraging them to attack us.'

In the aftermath, Zulu labourers started coming to

Mdukatshani at night to warn Neil that their masters were planning murder. One alleged plot was for a sniper to take out Neil on a lonely road. Another was to lure him to a stock sale and start beating up a black in his presence; when Neil intervened in the fight, they'd kill him and claim justifiable homicide. Neil shrugged off the danger but some of his friends were worried. It was all too easy to see him slain by the bullet from an assassin's gun. Everyone knew, of course, where the danger lay, but when the shot finally rang out, it came from an entirely different direction.

8

The house of Qamatha Sokhela stood on a barren plain in the sun-blasted devastation of Msinga, half-way between Mdukatshani and the dusty hamlet of Tugela Ferry. Sokhela was an old man who had worked on the railways all his life. It was a good job and he became very rich, rich enough to afford three wives and a fine house, with five big rooms, brick walls, cement floors, glass windows and a tin roof. Inside, it was furnished with ancient Victorian armchairs and real beds, just like a white man's home. In Msinga terms, Sokhela's house was a mansion, but that was not why the neighbours envied the old man. They envied him because his roof could not be set alight and because bullets could not pass through his walls as they could through those of the mud huts of lesser men. In Msinga, Sokhela's house doubled as a fortress and that is why, at dawn on Christmas morning in 1982, its floors were covered with the sleeping forms of refugees—women and children who were too scared to sleep in their own huts because of the war.

The house of Sokhela overlooked a dry watercourse called the Hyena River. The land on Sokhela's side belonged to an *isigodi* called Mhlangaan. The land on the far side belonged to the Ndlela. In 1982, the Mhlangaan were at war with the Ndlela and the enemy was strong. The enemy sometimes raided the territory of the Mhlangaan at night, shooting up huts with sub-machine-guns and setting fire to their straw roofs. Women and children were usually considered non-combatants but they still risked being caught in the cross-fire in these nocturnal raids. So dozens of them slept in Sokhela's house for safety. Their fathers, husbands and brothers were in the hills fighting. They had been up there for three months, living 'like baboons' in the ravines. Old Sokhela had been in the hills himself but he was now too old to fight, too old even to run when it became necessary. Some black policemen from Tugela Ferry caught him and ordered him to reveal the hiding-place of the Mhlangaan army. But Sokhela did not trust the police, fearing that they would betray the whereabouts of his brothers to the Ndlela. When he refused to speak, the policemen beat him with their rifle butts and he was hurt inside. So he came down from the hills on Christmas Eve and slept in his own house. It was his plan to rise at dawn and flee the district.

Just before the sun rose, however, the slumbering refugees were awakened by the sound of gunfire. One of Sokhela's daughters opened the door and peered outside. She heard shouts. She heard doors kicked open at the neighbouring kraal. She heard the wail of an old woman whose husband had been shot dead as he hunted a lost cow in the grey dawn. And then she saw them: 'many, many' black men, wearing uniforms and military caps and carrying rifles. It was the Ndlela *impi*, the Ndlela army. By now, the refugees knew there was danger coming. They were streaming out of the house and slipping away into the bush. Sokhela's daughter ran inside and woke her father. 'The war has come,' she said.

Sokhela hid under his bed. The daughter positioned herself in the doorway to await the enemy. She left the door open behind her, hoping to convey the impression that the house was empty. A Ndlela warrior sauntered towards her.

'Where is the man from here?' he asked.

'There is no man here,' she replied.

The soldier glanced through the door behind her, shrugged and turned to leave. Just then, however, old Sokhela moved in his hiding-place and the bed scraped on the cement floor. The Ndlela soldier turned back. 'Come, come,' he shouted to his comrades, 'there is someone here.' Several Ndlela soldiers pushed the daughter aside and stormed into the house, rifles at the ready. 'I came away,' she told me, 'because I didn't want to see. They have come to kill my father and I don't want to see.'

The bullets passed through the mattress and into Sokhela's heart, and he became the fifth casualty in another of Msinga's senseless wars. Why had he died? An ancient elder of Sokhela's faction dimly remembered a land dispute, but he could not say exactly how it originated or when, because it had happened long before his time. Otherwise, Mhlangaan's warriors said the war arose from an incident that had taken place in a migrant workers' barracks in the distant city of Kimberley in 1965.

'It all started,' said Masithela Mbatha, an elder from Mhlangaan, 'when a young man named Ntsele was sitting quietly and drinking his beer. Two men from Ndlela sat down with him and helped themselves to his beer. Ntsele said: "How can you drink my beer without asking?" And the Ndlela men said: "How can you stop us?" ' Ntsele was from Mhlangaan and he told his 'brothers' about this rudeness. The insult festered for weeks. 'Then Christmas came,' Masithela continued, 'and all we Zulus gathered for a beer-drink. Everyone was discussing this thing that was done to Ntsele and the young men wanted to fight. I was there. I fought, too. We fought with sticks and spears and knives. Five men were killed—four of them and one of us.'

The men involved in that brawl were arrested but released for lack of evidence. Once set free, they returned to Msinga and continued the war in the hills. 'Many' men were killed but the fires of anger finally burned out and peace returned to the banks of the Hyena River. By 1982, however, a new generation of warriors had come of age in Ndlela and they were thirsting for vengeance. They said, 'You killed our fathers in Kimberley, so we must kill you.'

The new war started quietly, as these wars do. A Mhlangaan man was assassinated in Johannesburg. In Msinga, a Ndlela was killed in retaliation. One night, the Ndlela army came into Mhlangaan and shot up a kraal with machine-guns. After that, the men on either side took to the hills with their guns and the war got underway in earnest. In the ensuing nine months, it claimed twenty-one lives, including Bokhela's. Three men were assassinated in hostels in Johannesburg, one in Dundee. Two were killed in a shoot-out aboard a bus. Stezi Mpungose, a friend of Neil's, was ambushed on a footpath, shot dead and beheaded. The police made some half-hearted attempts to stop the war. A local chief intervened but he failed, too.

And then one day in the winter of 1983, two old men came down from the mountain to speak to Neil. Albert Mbatha was a jocular fellow whose trademark homburg was always tilted at a jaunty angle. Thobola Mutwa was a shy, diffident man who had recently retired after forty years in Johannesburg, where he had worked as a security guard. They were both good friends of Neil's, but he hadn't seen them for a long time. They had been on *impi*, active service in the ravines, for 300 nights and days. And now they were too old and tired to continue. 'Oh, *Numyaan*,' cried Albert, 'you must help us stop this killing.'

This was the truly tragic aspect of Msinga's wars: nobody wanted them, save the bloodthirsty young hotheads who set them off. Ordinary people thirsted for peace and stability. Hardly anyone wanted to fight, but older men like Albert found it hard to control their sons. 'When we tell them this terrible thing must stop,' he said, 'they reply, "Watch it, *baba* [father]. We'll hit you too."' So the youngsters stirred up trouble and then everyone else was forced to join in by the law of indiscriminate retaliation. Once the slaughter was under way, there was simply no mechanism to stop it. The tribal chief's power was waning and the South African Police were entirely ineffectual. Even if a killing took place in broad daylight within sight of hundreds, they could never seem to find witnesses. Maybe they didn't really try. It was said to cost about a hundred dollars to buy yourself out of a murder rap at the police station in Tugela Ferry, a goat or two for a lesser offence.

And now Albert and Mutwa were asking Neil for help. A less courageous man would have said 'No' on the spot. It was terribly dangerous to intervene in Msinga's disputes, but Neil never said 'No'. After the old men left, he contacted the police, the local chiefs and the district magistrates and started organizing a peace conference. At the time, there were two wars under way within a six-mile radius of the project—Mhlangaan versus Ndlela and Mashunka against Ngubo—and Neil decided to attempt settlements of both simultaneously. The preliminaries took three months. Warriors on all sides were suspicious and had to be convinced that they would not be assassinated if they came out of hiding. To allay their fears, Neil persuaded a police brigadier to give his blessing to the conference and to send some of his men to attend. It was a token gesture but it strengthened the warriors' confidence and a date was finally set.

On the appointed day, Bob Frean of Durban's *Daily News*

drove out to Msinga. The peace conference was the first of its kind and his paper thought it would make a fine feature story. Frean arrived at the project just after dawn and found Neil already waiting, dressed as usual in frayed jeans and car-tyre sandals.

In the newsman's estimation, the day got off to an inauspicious start. He and Neil climbed into the project's Japanese microbus and set out for a rendezvous, where a delegation from one of the warring factions was supposed to be waiting. The spot was deserted, so they waited.

Hours passed. The sun rose higher in the sky and the heat grew suffocating. The dusty hills shimmered and danced in the distance. Half-naked herdboys settled in the shade of nearby thorn trees and stared at the white men. Bony cattle hobbled by. Frean got out and walked around in the dust and desolation. He peered over the wall of a concrete stock dam and saw a dead dog floating in the scummy water. A crushing sense of enervation descended on him. Three hours in Msinga and he already wanted to get out. Alcock had been there eight years but he still wasn't complaining. In fact, he was sitting behind the wheel of the microbus, scribbling furious letters to newspapers and Members of Parliament about deplorable conditions in Msinga. Frean shook his head. How on earth did the man stand it?

Another person who had his doubts about what Neil was up to was Warrant-Officer Jurgen Freese of the firearm squad at Tugela Ferry. He was waiting in the town's sweltering court-house, fanning himself and yawning. In Jurgen Freese's opinion, the peace conference was a waste of time. He knew what would happen. The warriors would eventually arrive. Alcock would make a speech. Then the tribesmen would yell at one another about incidents that had taken place in their fathers' and grandfathers' days, and nothing would be resolved.

Freese was more or less right. In due course, all four delegations pitched up and Neil made some opening remarks. 'All of you are suffering,' he told the warriors. 'For months you have been sleeping on the hills. You have known the pain of having your friends and relatives killed. But the pain has to be forgotten if we are to find a path to stop the blood.' With that, he ceded the floor to the warriors.

One by one, they stood up to affirm that they, too, wanted peace, but beyond that, they found no common ground. 'A lot was spoken,' Freese commented, 'but nothing was really said.' In the end, the Zulus agreed only to meet again and the conference broke up on a note of anti-climax.

Outside, the heat was pitiless. Neil sent someone to buy cold drinks at the general store. The conferees waited on the shady porch of the court-house, watching goats forage through garbage in the dusty market-place across the street. Mutwa, Albert and other members of the Mhlangaan delegation stood on one side, the men of Ndlela on the other, not talking or even looking at one another. Later, people would claim to have seen sinister comings and goings around the court-house, conspiratorial nods and winks, but nobody remarked on them then, and besides, Neil was not really on the lookout for danger. He doubted that the Zulus would harm him. He was their brother, their father. That was what many called him—*uBabawethu*, our father.

Around four that afternoon, nineteen sweating Zulu men squeezed into Neil's microbus and set off for home. Neil took the road that peeled off the tar on the far side of the bridge and headed north along the banks of the river, towards the land of the Ndlelas. This was of no particular concern to those of his passengers who were members of the Mashunka faction, for they had no quarrel with the Ndlelas. The Mhlangaan men, on the other hand, fell dead silent as they entered the territory of their enemies. They were right to be afraid. Eyes were watching through binoculars. Word was passing down the line. Rifle bolts were snapping and clips of ammunition clicking into place on sub-machine-guns.

Half-way through the danger zone, the road ahead disappeared into a tumble of huge boulders. As the van neared the spot, some small Zulu boys at the roadside started dancing in a frenzy of excitement. The sight filled the passengers with alarm but Neil didn't seem to notice. His eyes were on the road.

As he turned the corner, some fifty to seventy Ndlela warriors rose from their hiding-places among the boulders and started shooting, concentrating their fire on the driver. A bullet from an automatic rifle hit Neil in the neck. Blood spewed into the windshield. The van slowed to a halt. Neil opened the door, staggered out and fell.

Behind him, Zulus were boiling out of the bus with bullets whistling around their ears. The neutral Mashunka delegation stood to one side with their hands up, screaming, '*Tshwele baThembu!*'—'Have mercy! Have mercy!' The Ndlela soldiers ignored them and fired at the fleeing Mhlangaan. Several were already injured—one hobbling away on a shattered foot, another trying to run while holding in his intestines with his hands. The Ndlelas left their hiding-places and gave chase, firing as they ran. The screams and gunshots died away in the distance and there was silence save for the groaning of the wounded. A Zulu man lay dying in the bus and four others—Mutwa and Albert among them—had been killed before getting very far. And Neil was lying on his face in the dust of Africa, dead.

Once the shooting stopped, crowds of weeping, praying Zulu women converged on the scene. They found an old Zulu man sitting bleakly in the middle of the road, keeping watch over Neil's body. As Neil fell, his briefcase burst open, scattering papers and money. Someone suggested that the old man pick up the papers, but he said no. The police must see it all, just as it happened; nothing must be touched. So he fetched a rock, placed it beside Neil's body and sat down upon it, waiting.

One or two cars came by, but their black drivers were too scared to help. A big bus thundered over the horizon in a cloud of dust, edged through the crowd, past Neil's body, and drove on without stopping. The sun wheeled and set, and it was nightfall when the police came.

The old man looked up and saw cigarettes glowing in the dark above him. One of the cops stirred Neil's corpse with his toe.

'We don't pick up dogs,' he said. 'You pick him up. He's your Jesus.'

9

And so Neil was dead. For many days, it did not seem real to Creina. Zulu women started brewing beer and preparing food for a funeral. Whose funeral? An old black man appeared in the doorway, took off his hat and held it over his heart. 'You're all alone now,' he said, 'all alone, all alone.' It all seemed so unreal.

One morning while it was still dark outside, she heard the clink of shovels and spades as men climbed the hill to dig the grave. Later, she heard the big truck start and knew her stepson Dave had left to fetch the bodies from Greytown. They had been taken there, forty miles away in white South Africa, because there were rumours of a plot to steal the corpses from the morgue at Tugela Ferry and dismember them for inclusion in a battle-medicine brew. So Dave drove all the way to Greytown and when he got there the police declined to release all six bodies to him, citing talk of a plot to waylay the truck on its way back into Msinga. And so only Neil's body was taken from the morgue and placed in its coffin, a reject bought cheap from an undertaker in the Place of Weeping. The coffin was loaded on the truck and set out on its last sad journey, bracketed by vehicles bristling with armed police.

Neil had asked to be buried on the cliff-top, on a spot overlooking the bend in the river and the sweeping flood-plain beyond. A crowd was waiting up there in the burning sun—two prominent black men in suits and a thousand ordinary Msinga people in rags and tatters and vestiges of tribal finery. Many mourners remarked favourably on the coffin, which was made of two shades of wood, one light and the other dark. They said it was a fitting coffin for a man like Neil Alcock, who was half-black and half-white in his heart.

An ancient Zionist prophet said a few words and the crowd sang 'Nkosi Sikalel iAfrika', 'God Bless Africa'. And then the coffin was lowered into the grave and covered with stones, and Creina turned and walked away. She sat near the river for a while, watching the male mourners wind down the cliff to the flat rocks at its base, where they stripped off their clothes and washed themselves in accordance with Zulu burial ritual. This is not real, she thought; this is not my river; it looks just like the Ganges.

And so Neil was dead. Why? It seemed so pointless for him to have died in that way. In the distant cities, many whites received the news with disbelief, thinking: No, this just can't be; Neil Alcock cannot have been killed by Zulu. They were certain that there must have been a conspiracy, that if the connections could only be traced, it would emerge that the order for the killing came from somewhere inside the white system, inside the secret police or the apparatus of military intelligence. All the laws of destiny, the rules of poetic symmetry and the requirements of plot demanded that this be so, but there was little to back up the theory save its proponents' longing to believe it. It was hard to believe that any white man other than Neil himself had sufficient influence among the tribes to coax an *impi* to do his secret bidding.

The bad-cop theory was a little more compelling. Shortly before his death, Neil had finally prevailed on the police brass to send an undercover officer to investigate Msinga's hundreds of unsolved murders and the reek of fix that hung over them. In the weeks leading up to the ambush, Neil and a policeman named Fires van Vuuren held several secret meetings with Zulus who claimed to have evidence regarding such things. Under the circumstances, certain members of the police garrison at Tugela Ferry had reason to wish Neil dead and they were in a position to have organized it—most of them were Zulu, several with blood ties to the Ndlela faction.

The mystery was never really solved, although the police seemed to try a little harder than usual. Alcock was a *kafferboetie* and a perpetual pain in their necks, but he remained a white man and killing him an act of *lèse-majesté* that called for swift and certain retribution. So police poured into the district, set up a tent camp on the outskirts of Tugela Ferry and used helicopters to round up the Ndlela *impi*. Scores of warriors were arrested and a dozen or so weapons dug up from secret caches in the bush. Ballistics tests proved that some of the guns had been used in the ambush, but the police apparently struggled to establish exactly whom they belonged to and by whom their triggers had been pulled.

Eventually, thirteen Ndlelas were charged with murder, but there wasn't much of a case against them. Six men were shot dead in broad daylight on an open road in a densely populated area but nobody saw anything. It was the same old Msinga story. Indeed, the case differed from the thousands before it in only one respect—there was at least one witness, a woman named Buthelezi who stepped forward and broke the law of silence. She told the police she had seen a throng of men with rifles at the ready sitting on the rocks above the ambush site an hour before the killings. She identified eighteen of them by name and then she vanished. When I went looking for her, some Zulus told me there was no such person and never had been. A white policeman interpreted this to mean she was probably dead. Without her, there was no case at all; the attorney-general declined to prosecute and the thirteen suspects were set free.

So white man's justice had failed yet again and to some men in the valley the situation seemed to call for a traditional Msinga solution. Soon after the ambush, the generals of four nearby *isigodi* came to Creina and told her that if she wished, if she was hungry for blood, they would lead their combined armies into Ndlela and burn it to the ground. Creina thanked them, for they were paying her dead husband a great honour, but said 'No.' Neil would not have wanted more war. So the generals went home and the case was closed in Msinga terms, too. All that was left was for Creina to come to terms with it, and that was the hardest part of all.

She believed in love, you see; not in a sentimental sense, or a religious sense, but just . . . love: giving of yourself and trying to do good for others. Her and Neil's willingness to love had carried them deeper into Africa than any other whites and she thought love would protect them there. It seemed she had been mistaken. 'After Neil's death,' she said, 'I thought that the whole of my life had been meaningless, and that I had misunderstood every single thing I had ever looked at—that there had never been any meaning from the beginning.'

After thinking it through, Creina concluded that she must somehow have failed in love, not loved enough or sacrificed enough to shield her husband from the forces at work in Msinga. It seemed to her that staying was the only way to salvage the meaning of Neil's life, so she refused to abandon the project. Friends, relatives and the police tried to convince her otherwise, but she refused. 'Have you ever planted a tree?' she asked one policeman. 'Neil and I planted a tree and I must stay to see it grow.' The chorus of white friends and relatives eventually gave up and returned to their cities, leaving Creina and her teenaged sons on their own.

She built a rock garden on Neil's grave and planted it with aloes, wild flowers and grasses. She sat on the grave for hours on end, all through the night sometimes, telling herself that the world had not come to a standstill, that life and movement remained; that even sitting there, in the hollow she had worn on her husband's grave, she was hurtling through space at 900 miles an hour. She grew thin and gaunt, and her friends sometimes feared for her sanity, for she was in the habit, in that extremity of grief, of talking about Neil in the present tense, as if he were still alive. They redoubled their efforts to persuade her to leave, but she would have none of it. 'Every time I left the farm I felt as though I was dying,' she said. 'It was the only reality there was, and the world outside was so strange.'

A year passed, a bitterly hard year for a white woman alone in Africa and a widow at that, so low on the African social scale that she had virtually ceased to exist. Creina couldn't speak Zulu very well and knew next to nothing about farming—Neil had always taken care of that. In fact, Neil had taken care of almost everything and now Neil was gone. 'The centre-pole has fallen,' said the Zulus, referring to the pole that kept their structures of mud and thatch erect. They doubted that the project could survive without him and doubted that Creina had the courage to stay. Believing that Mdukatshani was doomed, some of them started taking care of their own interests. There was a rash of petty thefts. One of Neil's Zulu lieutenants ploughed and planted crops in a sacrosanct conservation camp. Another set himself up in the transport business, ferrying goods and people all over the district in the project's truck. A third man, also a truck driver, took to using the truck for his night-time jaunts. When Creina asked him to stop, he suggested she mind her own business.

And then someone entered Creina's office, which was never locked and could not in fact be locked, and took the only things of value in it: a broken cassette-recorder and a portable typewriter that Neil had given her. When the theft was discovered, everyone thought, Uh-oh, this is Mboma's doing—Mboma Dladla, the little Zulu starveling who'd become part of the Alcock household at the very beginning. Creina had nursed him back to health and he had become her son G. G.'s best friend and the subject of the best-selling *Story of a Herdboy*. Mboma and Ndudu and Sensilube—these are names we must resurrect now. They were among the herdboys who had once lived in her household and been her son's best friends—members of her family, virtually. Sensilube was the boy who milked the cows in secret so he could feed his orphaned brothers and sisters. Ndudu was the spiv, the boy with wit and sparkle, and Mboma was the clever one, the ingenious kid of whom Neil joked: 'This boy will either be prime minister or wind up on the gallows.'

Several years had since passed and Mboma, Ndudu and Sensilube were now in their late teens or early twenties. Ndudu and Sensilube were still living nearby, but Mboma had been cast out and it looked as though he was fulfilling the darker half of Neil's prophecy. He had been caught stealing from fellow Zulu workers and was kicked off the project at their insistence. Mboma's version was that he'd been framed and that the others had put a witchcraft on him because they were jealous of his closeness to Neil and the white boys. Whatever the truth, Mboma left the Alcocks and went to live with his father. The Alcocks heard that he'd dug up the old man's gun and sold it, then stolen his clothes and sold them, too. After that, Mboma was banished again and vanished into the maw of Soweto.

A few months after the ambush, though, he turned up in Msinga again. He'd grown into a heavy-set young man, moon-faced and slow-moving, with a con man's winning smile. The farm committee seemed to have forgotten that it had declared the project off-limits to him and Creina lacked the authority to enforce the rule herself. Whenever she drove out of the project's gates, there was Mboma, peering at her through his scholarly bifocals, thumb in the air for a ride. She always picked him up but she had grown wary of him from long experience. He was hanging around on the day her typewriter disappeared and the evidence pointed to him as the one who'd taken it.

Creina didn't think it worth calling the police, but the typewriter was of sentimental value, so she asked Mboma's community to help. A day or two later, two of Msinga's toughest guys showed up at the project, announcing that they'd come to solve the case of the missing typewriter. Kunene was a professional car-thief and Zwane a famous warrior, with many killings to his name. 'A most enchanting man,' said Creina, and not at all sarcastically; if you were prissy about choosing friends in Msinga, you were likely to have no friends at all. The two tough guys borrowed one of the project's vans and set out in search of Mboma.

That evening, Creina was flagged down in the bush by a crowd of shouting Zulu men. They told her they'd caught Mboma and

Sensilube, another of her Zulu sons, in possession of something in a suitcase. Was this the missing machine? It was indeed. Creina burst out crying. The Zulu men stood around beaming. It was just a small thing, but it gave Creina a tremendous surge of hope and confidence. By rallying around her, the Zulu men seemed to be saying that she, too, was an insider now, in the way that Neil had been.

Even as the hand-over ceremony was under way, however, Mboma and Sensilube were on their way to the police station at Tugela Ferry, to report that Zwane had levelled a revolver at them. Next thing, the police were out looking for him, investigating a firearms charge. Zwane fled to Johannesburg. As soon as he was out of the way, Mboma and Sensilube came swaggering back into the project, not in the least put out. When next Creina passed through the farm gates, Mboma was there as usual, smiling and chattering as though nothing had happened. There was little Creina could do but smile back and stop to pick him up.

Another year passed. One day, South Africa's minister of justice passed overhead in a helicopter and landed at Tugela Ferry, where a press conference was held. The minister made noises about cleaning up the district and ameliorating its suffering, but the killings continued, as did the hunger and hardship. Lacking Neil's command of Zulu and his male authority, Creina found it hard to negotiate the tortuous tribal politics on the far side of the river. She and the farm committee thus decided to expand the community gardens that lay on Mdukatshani itself. Several hundred additional plots were laid out alongside the river, dams built, a pump installed and the women of the valley invited in to till and hoe and plant. The gardens were a great success and Creina's bead business was doing better than ever. Orders were pouring in from the great fashion houses of Europe. Msinga beads were to be seen in the display cases of Yves St. Laurent, around the necks of *Vogue* models and on the wrists of Hollywood stars.

Bead day came once a month. On its eve, Creina drove into Greytown and drew the proceeds of sales from a bank. The following morning, Zulu women in purple cloaks and ochre head-dresses came out of the hills and, folding their stiff leather skirts beneath their thighs, settled in a great chattering flock in the shade of a big thorn tree. Creina sat down among them with a pair of scales and bags of ruby-red and aquamarine and emerald-green glass beads. Then loose beads were exchanged for finished articles and other things were exchanged, too: gossip and rumours of war, obituaries and requiems for newly dead fathers, husbands and sons. Creina loved her bead women and assumed they loved her back.

On the eve of one bead day, Creina's son came home from town with a vanload of bread and groceries and a satchel containing 2,000 dollars in cash—the bead women's wages. It was dark by the time they arrived, so they left the money and goods in the van overnight. In the morning, the petrol tank was empty and so was the vehicle itself: all the groceries had vanished, along with the satchel of cash.

Creina couldn't work out how the thief or thieves had carried off an entire vanload of loot on foot. She was standing there, puzzling it over, when some staff members mentioned that they'd just seen Mboma Dladla on the road, pushing a broken-down pick-up piled with cardboard cartons and grocery bags. Creina put two and two together and called the police. It turned out that Mboma's pick-up had been stolen in a nearby white town, and as for the missing groceries, some were discovered stashed away in his grandmother's kraal, along with about 180 dollars in cash. The rest of the money had vanished. 'What money?' said Mboma. 'I don't know what you're talking about.'

So Mboma was taken away, protesting his innocence, and Creina was left in a quandary. Forty or fifty Zulu women were sitting under the thorn tree outside her hut waiting to be paid for their beadwork. Creina felt rotten. She felt she'd been negligent and blamed herself for the theft. So she drove into town, borrowed money to cover the wages and resigned herself to the long and hard struggle of repaying the loan out of her own wage of seventy-five dollars a month.

There was some consolation to be drawn from the fact that Mboma was behind bars, and presumably on his way to jail, but it didn't last long. One Sunday, six weeks after his arrest, he came back home, laughing his head off again. Creina was outraged. She called the police, who explained that Mboma had been released because he had 'a sore eye'. Such were the mysterious processes of law enforcement in Msinga.

Mboma hadn't held a steady job in his life, but he suddenly seemed to have plenty of money. He tossed coins to adoring young herdboys, donated groceries to the poor. Indeed, someone claimed to have seen him root under a rock near his family's kraal and emerge with fistfuls of cash, which he threw into the air, singing and dancing and blessing his ancestors for bringing him luck. When asked where the money came from, Mboma reportedly laughed. 'If you are walking to water,' he said, 'and find something in your path, it is yours to keep.'

Creina tried not to count betryals. She'd virtually raised that boy. She provided a steady income for one of his grandmothers, who did beadwork, and Neil had lied to help his grandfather obtain a government old-age pension. She and Neil had done several good works in Mboma's community, which was Ndlela—the community whose army had ultimately murdered Neil. Indeed, one of Mboma's uncles was in the *impi* that carried out the killings, and when the police came hunting in helicopters, relatives used Creina's telephone to arrange a hiding-place in the city for him. Only one woman in Ndlela had come forward to testify about the ambush, and now nobody would testify about the bead-money theft—not even Creina's beloved bead women. Worse yet, Mboma emerged from the affair as something of a hero. Little Zulu boys would come to Creina and say, 'Oh, Mboma's so nice; he's giving us presents,' while their mothers stood around beaming. What could Creina do? She forgave, as she'd always forgiven.

From a criminal point of view, the theft of the bead money was inspirational. In Msinga, 2,000 dollars was a fortune. Nobody in the valley had had any idea that there were such riches on Mdukatshani, to be had more or less for the taking. In Msinga, anyone who owned anything worth stealing had guns, guards and barbed-wire fences, but Creina was alone and defenceless.

One night, she was awakened by a torch in her face. Two young black men were standing over her bed, levelling a revolver at her. 'We want money,' they said. 'We kill you.' Creina got up and opened the safe where the bead women's wages were kept. She was a little too slow for the robbers' liking, so they clubbed her to the ground with the butt of the gun, then hauled her to her feet, bleeding and half-conscious, and warned her to be quick about it. So she handed over the package of banknotes and they vanished into the night.

She didn't know who had done it, of course, and Ndudu was the last person she suspected. Ndudu was one of her younger son's best friends. He was no longer working on the project but he almost always came to lunch on Sunday. He was there as usual after the robbery, full of solicitude, and wondering aloud who could have done such a vile deed. He knew more than he was letting on, though. He knew when Creina went to get the money, how much it was and where she hid it. He also knew her dogs. A day or two later, he was in police custody, confessing that it was he who led the robbers to the house, he who calmed the barking dogs and held them while his accomplices went inside to pistol-whip his white mother.

After Ndudu's robbery, the darkness seemed to close in on Creina. If Mboma, Sensilube and Ndudu were not loyal to her, was there anyone in the valley whom she could trust? Suddenly, every sign seemed ominous. Strangers approached the project's staff asking curious questions about her dogs. The telephone kept ringing in the dead of night and a black voice would ask for people she'd never heard of. For the first time in her life, Creina grew afraid. She came to dread the sunset. She often lay awake long into the night, listening for footfalls on the path outside her hut, and praying that if they came again, they would at least not hit her, please not hit her. Half of her face was left nerveless after Ndudu's robbery and she'd almost lost an eye.

And then the year turned, and it was 1985. The winter was a bad one, as brutal as any in recent memory. By August, it had not rained in ten months. The grass was all eaten and cattle started dying again. Even the rats grew desperate—so desperate that they lost their fear of humans and started invading Msinga's houses. At night, when Creina doused her lamp, they invaded her hut and skittered over her face as she lay waiting for the next Ndudu.

When the sun rose, the sky was blue and cold and cloudless, and puffs of powdery dust hung in the wake of bony cattle moving on the hillsides. And then the goats started coming, huge swarms of hungry goats, pouring through holes in the project's cut fences and devouring every last shred of vegetation on Mdukatshani's dusty, eroded hills. The goat-owners lived along the project's boundaries and Creina regarded them as friends. She begged them to keep their animals out and they were only too eager to oblige. For a day or two, there would be no goats on the project, but promises were soon forgotten and the goats would come again, scavenging along the river bank and right into Creina's mud-walled living-room. She'd come home at night to find dung on her windowsills, dung all over the floor.

Creina was so weary of talking. She and Neil and their Zulu allies had talked nicely for more than a decade, but nothing ever seemed to change. It had started with the cattle rustling, back in 1975. Neil had solved that problem by getting rid of the co-operative's cattle and negotiating a grazing accord. Zulu stock-owners were supposed to work one day a month on land reclamation projects in return for each beast on Mdukatshani's land. Some Zulus had failed to live up to their side of the bargain, however, and when no action was taken against them, many of the rest followed suit. They saw no reason why they should work for grazing when the next man got it free.

And then drought came and the grazing accord collapsed entirely. Zulus knew that Neil would never shoot them or impound their cattle, as other whites did, so the project's fences were cut to ribbons and Zulu cattle let loose on the project's land. By the end of the first dry winter, more than a thousand Zulu cattle and innumerable goats were trespassing on the project, and Mdukatshani was living up to its name: a place of lost grasses.

Still, Neil understood why this was happening. He understood the Zulus' love for cattle and the desperation that drove them to such acts. So he forgave, as he'd always forgiven. That became a little harder the following year. The drought eased a little, but livestock trespass continued and there was little Neil could do about it—little anyone could do, short of resorting to force. Neil's two closest Zulu allies, his blood brothers Majozi and Nxongo, had recently became chief *induna*s or prime ministers of their respective Zulu sub-tribes. Both men urged their people to co-operate with the project; both were warned to mind their own business or die. As if to underscore the threats, a Zulu man appointed to make sure that no green trees were felled on Mdukatshani was waylaid and beaten to within an inch of his life.

By the time the drought entered its third year, Neil had become desperate—so desperate that he and his Zulu allies decided to emulate their white neighbours and conduct a cattle round-up of their own. The idea was to drive the trespassing stock to the kraal of the nearest Zulu chief and ask him to try and punish the faithless stock owners under traditional law. The posse never reached its destination, though. It was waylaid en route by a mob of irate Zulus who waved sticks in the air and howled with outrage, accusing the white man of stealing their cattle. They threatened violence and a very ugly scene ensued. Neil wound up firing warning shots into the air to keep the peace and had to let the trespassing goats and cattle go.

'There are two theories of fence maintenance,' Creina observed in her next newsletter. 'Shoot or negotiate. Our neighbours live by the first theory, we live by the second. Our neighbours have their fences cut, but Mdukatshani's fences are severed too. If guns, threat and talks have failed, what's left? Something formidably slow.'

Formidably slow indeed. In the final year of his life, Neil was reduced to pleading with the local Zulu chiefs to support the project and uphold some semblance of law. This put the chiefs in a very difficult position. Their own authority was growing tenuous and they were reluctant to be seen as acting against their own people on behalf of a project run by a white man. Shortly before his death, Neil asked Msinga's Regional Authority, or council of chiefs, to put the sensitive livestock trespass issue on the agenda for an upcoming meeting. On the appointed day, he spent four hours waiting at the meeting-place, but no chiefs came and Neil didn't live long enough to find out why. A week later, he was dead, shot down in broad daylight by Zulus, within earshot of hundreds of Zulus who heard nothing.

And now, in the winter of 1985, the situation was worse than ever. Whenever Creina raised her eyes to the horizon, goats were swarming across it. After they'd eaten everything else, they started on Neil's grave, stripping it of its flowers and grasses and defiling it with their droppings. 'I just felt desperate,' Creina said. 'We had meeting after meeting with everyone. I said, "For God's sake, can't you just make sure the goats don't get into the gardens?" They had finished my garden.

They finished everybody's gardens. Day after day, we'd see them coming from almost everywhere, advancing. I'd say to people, "Can't you just post children, just let them swim in the river and shoo the goats away?"' Small boys would be posted for a day or two, but then they'd vanish and the invasion would begin again.

Early one winter morning, Creina set out from her home with a pack of mongrels at her heels. One of the dogs was Insiswa, a tawny brute with the look of a jackal and an instinct to go for the throat. As a puppy, he'd attacked goats, but the habit had been thrashed out of him. He was a good dog these days. Creina led the dogs across the dirt road and up into the foothills, to a barren, sheet-eroded field she was trying to reclaim. She was working alone, laying rocks in anti-erosion contours, when the first flock of goats appeared. She waved her arms, shouted and threw pebbles at them. The goats scattered but as soon as Creina turned her back they returned. She chased them off several times but they always came back again.

Soon, two more flocks appeared. While she was chasing one, another would dash into the field behind her. The goats were pitiless, relentless. The skirmish went on all morning and it was slowly driving Creina mad. She thought she'd lost the ability to feel anger when Neil was murdered, but she was suddenly seething with rage. She thought: Well, maybe the only way anybody will understand anything is if I do things the way Msinga does.

Msinga's way was violence and killing, and Msinga's rules, as Creina saw them, were 'an eye for an eye, and then an arm for an arm, and a leg for a leg.' That was the law on the black side of the frontier, and on the white side of the frontier, too. If black-owned goats invaded a white man's land, the white man shot or impounded them and threatened to do likewise to their owners—to put a bullet between their eyes and throw their black bodies in a thorn thicket so dense that their rotting corpses would be traced only by the smell. This was an old Afrikaner philosophy called *kragdadigheid*, the act of power: You took what you wanted, and held it with your gun and fists. Creina and Neil Alcock had spent their entire lives fighting against whites who lived according to that barbaric philosophy, but now Creina decided to try it their way.

It was August 1985, almost two centuries since my ancestor Dawid Malan crossed the Great Fish River. Like him, Creina entered Africa an enlightened creature. Her head was full of reason and rationality, of D. H. Lawrence and T. S. Eliot. She was a gentle person, moved easily to tears. She was so sickened by violence that she could not bear to sit through an ordinary Hollywood action-adventure movie. She had always tried to love, but now it was time to kill.

When the next flock came, she whistled for Insiswa and took off running alongside the goats, inciting the dog to attack. Insiswa had been whipped for attacking goats, so he was bewildered and uncertain at first. Creina kept goading, though, and the dog finally took off on the hunt. Creina lost sight of him, but she heard a terror-stricken bleating in the bushes and knew he'd caught and killed a goat. Insiswa returned, tail wagging, and Creina was coldly pleased.

She set the dog on another goat, and then another, and another. Two goats were killed, two injured too badly to walk, before Creina decided that she had shed enough blood to make herself clear. Then she stalked over to the community gardens and told the Zulu women what she'd done. 'Insiswa has just killed your goats,' she shouted. 'It was not an accident. I wanted to kill them and will go on killing your goats until they stop coming on to the farm. Go home and tell your men!'

The following morning, Creina returned to the site of her killings and found one of the dead goats still lying there, half-eaten by some scavenging beast. She set to work, carrying rocks to and fro. The smell of death hung in the air around her. An old Zulu woman—a relative of Mboma's—came up to her, asking for blankets and food. Creina screamed, 'Go away, you horrible old woman!' She worked furiously all morning, entirely untroubled by goats. There wasn't a single goat on the project. Not one.

'I thought I had won,' Creina said. 'I had beaten Msinga. I had found a language Msinga could understand.'

As she spoke, we were sitting beside a dying fire in a bitterly cold mud hut. Creina had been talking into my tape-recorder every night for almost a week, and her voice had fallen to a hoarse whisper. Her tale was not yet done, but I covered my eyes and tried to stop listening. I was thinking about Dawid Malan and the Doppers, the ancient white frontiersmen who had extinguished the light of the Enlightenment because they found themselves in a place where love made men weak and doubtful. In Africa, as Creina said, it was an eye for an eye, then an arm for an arm, and a leg for a leg. If you loved, you were vulnerable, and if you were vulnerable you were weak, and if you were weak you got fucked, and fucked again, and again, and again, until you could no longer stand it. For this was not the end of Creina's torment.

The first death threat came about three weeks later and it brought home to Creina what she had done. It was like waking up from a bad dream, a nightmare in which some foul excrescence had come bubbling up out of some uncharted reach of her brain. She felt defiled. She had behaved like a savage, like a Boer—like all those white men along the border who shot or impounded trespassing Zulu livestock and threatened to do likewise to their owners. She felt as though she'd betrayed everything she lived for and all Neil had died for. So she prostrated herself before the aggrieved goat owner, begging forgiveness for her uncontrollable temper and promising to make restitution.

It was a mistake. It merely revealed another vulnerability, another avenue of exploitation. Not long after, Creina received a second letter in the post. In it, a Zulu man accused her of killing eight of his goats, in a place where she had never been. He demanded compensation and added a little postscript, entirely in keeping with the traditions of a brutal continent. 'If you don't pay,' he wrote, 'I will kill you.'

'I looked out of the door,' Creina whispered, 'and I was terribly afraid. I had this sense of utter blackness. I thought: Well, I can't actually live in Msinga, because I haven't got what it takes to live by Msinga rules. I could manage two goats once, but I would never be able to keep it up. I felt utterly betrayed by loving. All the things I had ever been told about love just weren't true. It was all full of false promises. I understood that love was a safety and a protection, and that if you loved you would be rewarded by someone loving you back, or at least not wanting to damage you. But it wasn't true, any of it. I knew that if I stayed, this was how it was going to be: it would never get any better; it would stay the same, or get worse. I thought: If you're really going to live in Africa, you have to be able to look at it and say: This is the way of love, down this road: Look at it hard. This is where it is going to lead you.

'I think you will know what I mean if I tell you love is worth nothing until it has been tested by its own defeat. I felt I was being asked to try to love enough not to be afraid of the consequences. I realized that love, even if it ends in defeat, gives you a kind of honour; but without love, you have no honour at all. I think that is what I had misunderstood all my life. Love is to enable you to transcend defeat.

'You said one could be deformed by this country, and yet it seems to me one can only be deformed by the things one does to oneself. It's not the outside things that deform you, it's the choices you make. To live anywhere in the world, you must know how to live in Africa. The only thing you can do is love, because it is the only thing that leaves light inside you, instead of the total, obliterating darkness.'

10

Creina Alcock is still living in Msinga. The wars continue as always, unreported by anyone. The village across the river was burned down one night and the view from Creina's bluff in the morning evoked Berlin at the end of World War Two. The drought of the early eighties gave way to a season of floods, one of which obliterated her home under a fifteen-foot-deep glacier of mud.

A while ago, gunmen came to the project to kill a Zulu headman staying there. They surrounded Creina's house, cut the telephone line and opened fire on the night-watchmen. Creina crawled out of a window and fled. In the darkness, she ran into a warrior who raised his rifle and pulled the trigger, twice. Hearing all this gunfire, the project's Zulu staff thought Creina was surely dead, but they found her alive in the morning, shivering in a hiding-place on the river's bank. Again, people who loved her tried to persuade her to leave but she remained determined to stay. 'Trust can never be a fortress,' she said, 'a safe enclosure against life. Trusting is dangerous. But without trust there is no hope for love, and love is all we ever have to hold against the dark.'

And it cannot be said that the Alcocks' love has gone unrewarded, in spite of all that has happened. The long years of struggle against desertification appear to be bearing fruit. There is grass where there was no grass before and the dongas are slowly silting over. Little Zulu children build anti-erosion contours with pebbles on footpaths. Their fathers have visions of a green valley not so different from the one Neil once saw. There is less tension along the border now. White farmers say it is because Alcock is no longer around to stir things up, but who knows—perhaps it is the memory of Neil's last crusade that stays their hands. There is a line of T. S. Eliot's that Creina is fond of quoting: *Be satisfied that ye have enough light to secure another foothold.* She has held on to a foothold in Africa and her husband's investment of love would seem to have been redeemed.

Early one morning in the winter of 1988, two ageing Zulu men who'd loved and honoured Neil climbed into a pick-up and drove to the bend in the road where he was killed. What they were about to do had never been done before and there were those Zulu traditionalists who thought it should not be done at all. They asked, 'How can you do this thing?' and the two men answered, 'Because Neil, he was same like a black man. The skin was white, but the heart it was same like a black.'

One of the Zulus was Petros Majozi, the man who'd given up his job and pension on the basis of a single glimpse into a white man's heart. The other was Majozi Nxongo, the tribal warrior-statesman who once helped me when I was a floundering white reporter. They stood over the spot where their white brother was slain and invited his spirit to enter their sacred stick. '*Numyaan,*' they said, 'we come to fetch you. Come, let us go to home.' Then they placed the stick in a plastic bag and returned in solemn silence to the mud house by the river, bringing Neil's spirit back home.

The following day, a huge crowd of Zulus gathered outside Creina's house, looking more ragged and pitiful than ever in honour of this great occasion. At such a ceremony, Zulus wore their oldest clothes, to ensure that the returning spirit would recognize them and not be startled by unfamiliar sights. There were several *sangoma*s in the crowd, draped in beads and totems, with inflated pig bladders in their hair and, right beside them, an old friend of Neil's from the townships—a black man in a jacket and tie, as fascinated by the strange goings-on as any of the whites present. Two cattle were brought forward and slaughtered with knives, in such a way that their bellowing might awaken and summon

110

Msinga's shades. Then the carcasses were butchered and hung in great bloody chunks in Creina's bedroom, which looked like a charnel house by the time the ceremony was done: blood on the walls, blood on the floor; blood to wash the sins and sorrows of the past away.

After that, the ceremony became a celebration and Zulus came from far and wide to join in. Two thousand litres of beer were drunk, mountains of food consumed and the dancing carried on for two days. And, finally, the horns of the sacrificial cattle were nailed to the thatched roof of Creina's hut, signalling that the household within had honoured its shades. In a continent where people worship their ancestors, Neil Alcock had become a god—the first white god in Africa, as far as anybody knows. Aeons after we left, the first white man had come home to Africa to stay.

THE
MEZZANINE
NICHOLSON BAKER

THE MEZZANINE is the story of one man's lunch hour. It addresses the big questions of corporate life in the grand manner:

Why does one shoe-lace always wear out before the other?
Whose genius lies behind the wing-flap spout on the milk carton?
Whatever happened to the paper drinking-straw?

'Easily the best first novel of 1988.'
The Boston Globe

'I love novels with gimmicks. By that I mean novels that are told not through plain old narrative but rather through some enormously complicated technical stunt. The list of great ones is not long; "Tristram Shandy" comes to mind, and Nabokov's brilliant "Pale Fire", a story told entirely in footnotes. Gimmick novels are often parodies, but this is not essential – just look at "Ulysses", which I consider the ultimate gimmick novel. "The Mezzanine", a first novel by Nicholson Baker, has no story, no plot, no conflict. When somebody describes it to you it sounds stupid (which, by the way, is a characteristic of all good gimmick novels). Yet its 135 pages probably contain more insight into life as we live it than anything currently on the best seller lists.'

The New York Times Book Review

Nicholson Baker lives in Mount Morris, New York, with his wife and child. His stories have appeared in *The Atlantic* and *The New Yorker*. This is his first novel.

On sale
from all good bookshops
price £10.95 (hardback)

PATRICK ZACHMANN

WALLED CITY

OF HONG KONG

The Walled City, Kowloon.

Patrick Zachmann

I first went to Kowloon's Walled City in 1987 with a Chinese friend. I returned there alone in the summer of last year.

When I saw the city from the outside I could not see an entrance; there seemed no way to get in. As I got closer I saw many small alleyways. Inside it was night. No sunlight reached the streets so it was night all day. Many people had umbrellas; the city was so humid that, although it was not raining outside, it was raining within.

We had a guide who was a member of one of the secret societies and slowly I came to understand how the complex world inside worked. The Chinese people always had a front. They were businessmen, professionals, but behind those identities they were running illegal activities for rival Triad groups, criminal organizations whose influence spreads throughout the island, and worldwide.

Gambling.

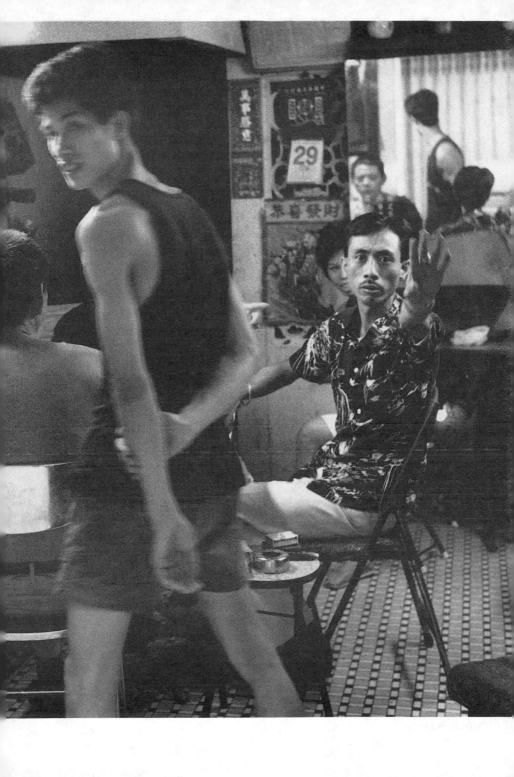

A police raid.

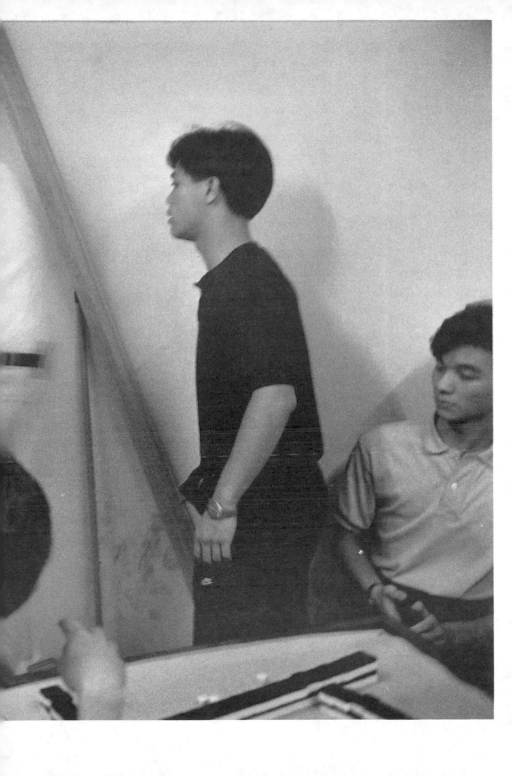

A woman hiding from the police.

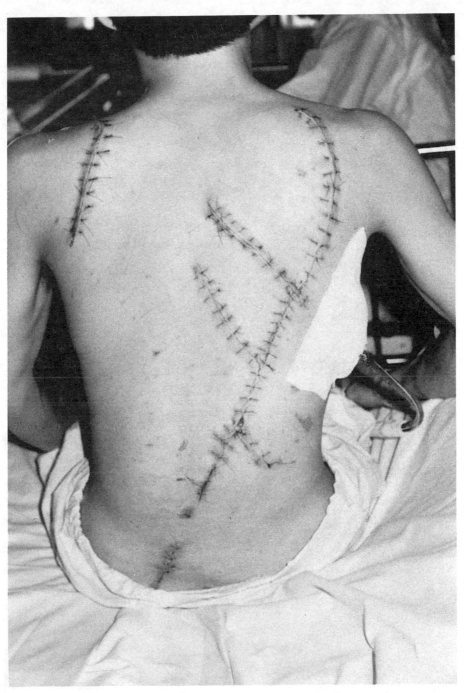

A Triad victim.

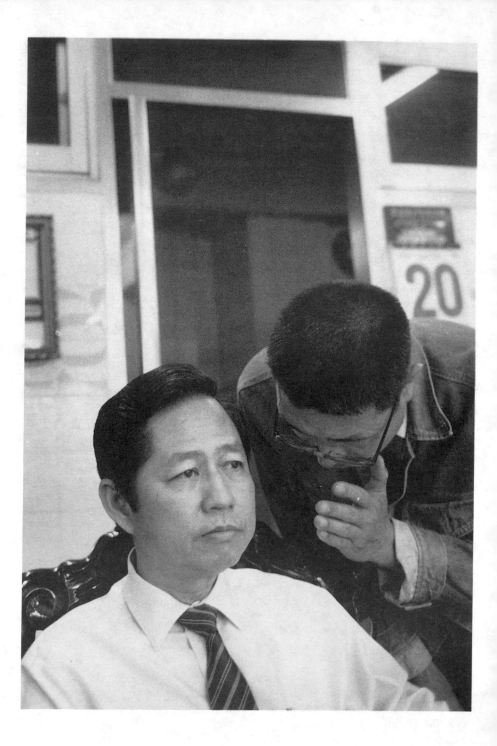

Opposite: A dentist. Above: Businessmen.

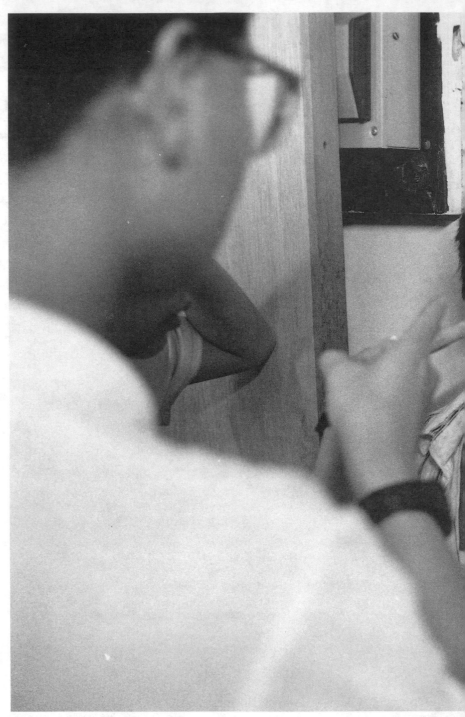

Police question a suspect.

Above and following pages: The red-light district of Wan Chi, Hong Kong.

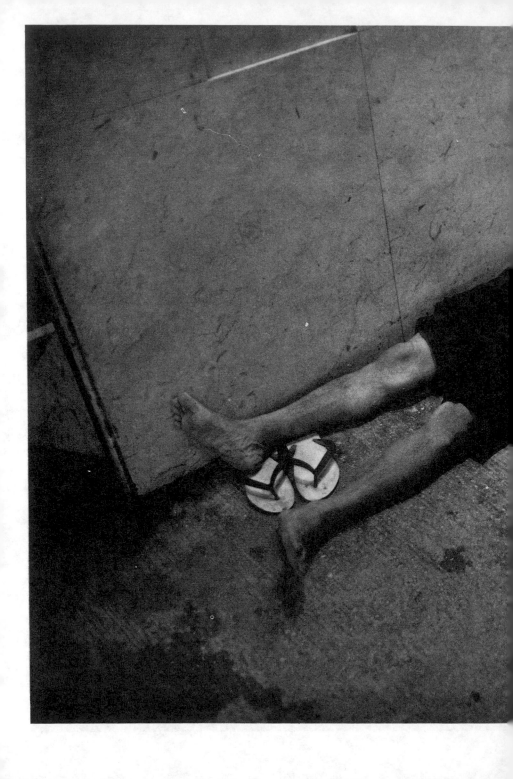

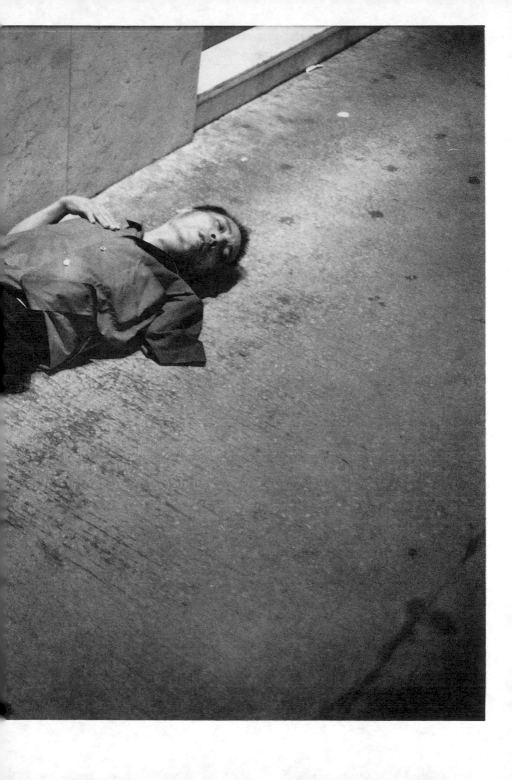

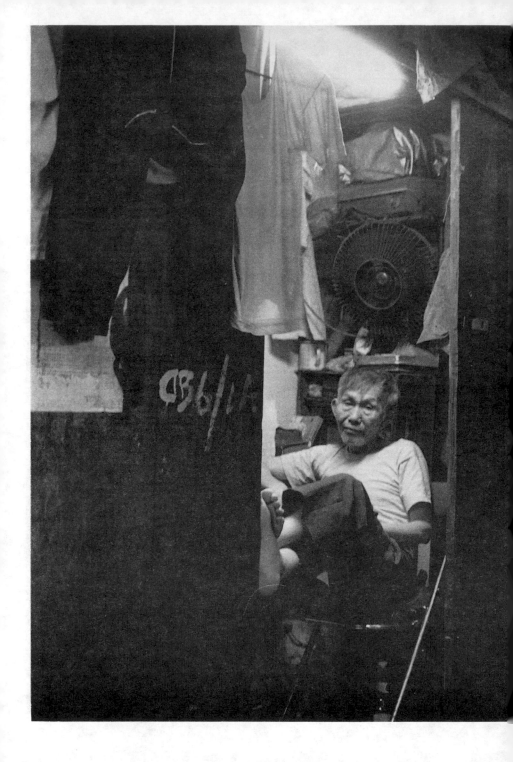

TIM O'BRIEN

SPEAKING

OF COURAGE

T he war was over and there was no place in particular to go. Norman Bowker followed the tar road on its seven-mile loop around the lake, then he started all over again, driving slowly, feeling safe inside his father's big Chevy, now and then looking out on the lake to watch the boats and water-skiers and scenery. It was Sunday and it was summer, and the town seemed pretty much the same. The lake lay flat and silvery against the sun. Along the road the houses were all low-slung and split-level and modern, with big porches and picture windows facing the water. The lawns were spacious. On the lake-side of the road, where real estate was most valuable, the houses were handsome and set deep in, well-kept and brightly painted, with docks jutting out into the lake, and boats moored and covered with canvas, and neat gardens, and sometimes even gardeners, and stone patios with barbecue spits and grills, and wooden shingles saying who lived where. On the other side of the road, to his left, the houses were also handsome, though less expensive and on a smaller scale and with no docks or boats or gardeners. The road was a sort of boundary between the affluent and the almost affluent, and to live on the lake-side of the road was one of the few natural privileges in a town of the prairie— the difference between watching the sun set over cornfields or over water.

It was a graceful, good-sized lake. Back in high school, at night, he had driven around and around it with Sally Kramer, wondering if she'd want to pull into the shelter of Sunset Park, or other times with his friends, talking about urgent matters, worrying about the existence of God and theories of causation. Then, there had not been a war. But there had always been the lake, which was the town's first cause of existence, a place for immigrant settlers to put down their loads. Before the settlers there were the Sioux, and before the Sioux there were the vast open prairies, and before the prairies there was only ice. The lake bed had been dug out by the southernmost advance of the Wisconsin glacier. Fed by neither streams nor springs, the lake was often filthy and algaed, relying on fickle prairie rains for replenishment. Still, it was the only important body of water within forty miles, a source of pride, nice to look at on bright summer days, and later that evening it would colour up with fireworks. Now, in the late afternoon, it lay calm and smooth, a good audience for silence, a seven-mile circumference that could be travelled by slow car in twenty-five minutes. It was not such a good lake for swimming. After college, he'd caught an ear infection that had almost kept him out of the war. And the lake had drowned his friend Max Arnold, keeping him out of the war entirely. Max had been one who liked to talk about the existence of God. 'No, I'm not saying *that*,' he'd argue against the drone of the engine, 'I'm saying it's possible as an *idea*, even necessary as an idea, a final cause in the whole structure of causation.' Now he knew, perhaps. Before the war, they'd driven around the lake as friends, but now Max was just an idea, and most of Norman Bowker's other friends were living in Des Moines or Sioux City, or going to school somewhere, or holding down jobs. The high school girls were mostly gone or married. Sally Kramer, whose picture he had once carried in his wallet, was one who had married. Her name now was Sally Gustafson and she lived in a pleasant blue house on the inexpensive side of the lake road. On his third day home he'd seen her out mowing the lawn, still pretty in a pink T-shirt and white shorts. For a moment he'd almost pulled over, just to talk, but instead he'd pushed down hard on the gas pedal. She looked happy. She had her house and her new husband, and there was really nothing he could say to her.

The town seemed remote somehow. Sally was married and Max was drowned and his father was at home watching baseball on national TV.

Norman Bowker shrugged. 'No problem,' he murmured.

Clockwise, as if in orbit, he took the Chevy on another seven-mile turn around the lake.

Even in late afternoon the day was hot. He turned on the air-conditioner, then the radio, and he leaned back and let the cold air and music blow over him. Along the road, kicking stones in front of them, two young boys were hiking with knapsacks and toy rifles and canteens. He honked going by, but neither boy looked up. Already he had passed them six times, forty-two miles, nearly three hours without stop. He watched the boys recede in his rear-view mirror. They turned a soft greyish colour, like sand, before finally disappearing.

He tapped down lightly on the accelerator.

Out on the lake a man's motorboat had stalled; the man was bent over the engine with a wrench and a frown. Beyond the stalled boat there were other boats, and a few water-skiers, and the smooth July waters, and an immense flatness everywhere. Two mud hens floated stiffly beside a white dock.

The road curved west, where the sun had now dipped low. He figured it was close to five o'clock—twenty after, he guessed. The war had taught him to tell time without clocks, and even at night, waking from sleep, he could usually place it within ten minutes either way. What he should do, he thought, was to stop at Sally's house and impress her with this new time-telling trick of his. They'd talk for a while, catching up on things, and then he'd say, 'Well, better hit the road, it's five thirty-four,' and she'd glance at her wrist-watch and say, 'Hey! How'd you *do* that?' and he'd give a casual shrug and tell her it was just one of those things you pick up. He'd keep it light. He wouldn't say anything about anything. 'How's it being married?' he might ask, and he'd nod at whatever she answered with, and he would not say a word about how he'd almost won the Silver Star for valour.

He drove past Slater Park and across the causeway and past Sunset Park. The radio announcer sounded tired. The temperature in Des Moines was eighty-one degrees, and the time was five thirty-five, and 'All you on the road, drive extra careful now on this fine Fourth of July.'

If Sally had not been married, or if his father were not such a baseball fan, it would be a good time to talk.

'The Silver Star?' his father might have said.

'Yes, but I didn't get it. Almost, but not quite.'

And his father would have nodded, knowing full well that many brave men did not win medals for their bravery, and that others won medals for doing nothing. As a starting-point, maybe, Norman Bowker might then have listed the seven medals he did win: the Combat Infantryman's Badge, the Air Medal, the Army Commendation Medal, the Good Conduct Medal, the Vietnam Campaign Medal, the Bronze Star, and the Purple Heart, though it wasn't much of a wound and did not leave a scar and did not hurt and never had. He would've explained to his father that none of these decorations were for uncommon valour. They were for common valour. The routine, daily stuff—just humping, just enduring—but that was worth something, wasn't it? Yes, it was. Worth plenty. The ribbons looked good on the uniform in his closet, and if his father were to ask, he would've explained what each signified and how he was proud of all of them, especially the Combat Infantryman's Badge, because it meant he had been there as a real soldier and had done all the things soldiers do, and therefore it wasn't such a big deal that he could not bring himself to be uncommonly brave.

And then he would have talked about the medal he did not win and why he did not win it.

'I almost won the Silver Star,' he would have said.

'How's that?'

'Just a story.'

'So tell me,' his father would have said.

Slowly then, circling the lake, Norman Bowker would have started by describing the Song Tra Bong. 'A river,' he would've said, 'this slow flat muddy river.' He would've explained how during the dry season it was exactly like any other river, nothing special, but how in October the monsoons began and the whole situation changed. For a solid month the rains never stopped, not once, and so after a few days the Song Tra Bong overflowed its banks and the land turned into a deep, thick muck for a half mile on either side. Just muck—no other word for it. Like quicksand, almost, except the stink was incredible. 'You couldn't even sleep,' he'd tell his father. 'At night you'd find a high spot, and you'd doze off, but then later you'd wake up because you'd be buried in all that slime. You'd just sink in. You'd feel it ooze up over your body and sort of suck you down. And the whole time there was that constant rain. I mean, it never stopped, not ever.'

'Sounds pretty wet,' his father would've said, pausing briefly. 'So what happened?'

'You really want to hear this?'

'Hey, I'm your *father*.'

Norman Bowker smiled. He looked out across the lake and imagined the feel of his tongue against the truth. 'Well, this one

time, this one night out by the river . . . I wasn't very brave.'
'You have seven medals.'
'Sure.'
'Seven. Count 'em. You weren't a coward either.'
'Well, maybe not. But I had the chance and I blew it. The stink, that's what got to me. I couldn't take that goddamn awful *smell*.'
'If you don't want to say any more—'
'I do want to.'
'All right then. Slow and sweet, take your time.'

The road descended into the outskirts of town, turning northwest past the junior college and the tennis courts, then past Chautauqua Park, where the picnic tables were spread with sheets of coloured plastic and where picnickers sat in lawn chairs and listened to the high school band playing Sousa marches under the band shell. The music faded after a few blocks. He drove beneath a canopy of elms, then along a stretch of open shore, then past the municipal docks where a woman in pedal-pushers stood casting for bullheads. There were no other fish in the lake except for perch and a few worthless carp. It was a bad lake for swimming and fishing, both.

He drove slowly. No hurry, nowhere to go. Inside the Chevy the air was cool and oily-smelling, and he took pleasure in the steady sounds of the engine and air-conditioning. A tour-bus feeling, in a way, except the town he was touring seemed dead. Through the windows, as if in a stop-motion photograph, the place looked as if it had been hit by nerve gas, everything still and lifeless, even the people. The town could not talk, and would not listen. 'How'd you like to hear about the war?' he might have asked, but the place could only blink and shrug. It had no memory, therefore no guilt. The taxes got paid and the votes got counted and the agencies of government did their work briskly and politely. It was a brisk, polite town. It did not know shit about shit, and did not care to know.

Norman Bowker leaned back and considered what he might've said on the subject. He knew shit. It was his speciality. The smell, in particular, but also the numerous varieties of texture and taste. Some day he'd give a lecture on the topic. Put on a suit and tie and stand up in front of the Kiwanis club and tell the fuckers about all the wonderful shit he knew. Pass out samples, maybe.

Smiling at this, he clamped the steering-wheel slightly right of centre, which produced a smooth clockwise motion against the curve of the road. The Chevy seemed to know its own way.

The sun was lower now. Five fifty-five, he decided—six o'clock, tops.

Along an unused railway spur, four workmen laboured in the shadowy red heat, setting up a platform and steel launchers for the evening fireworks. They were dressed alike in khaki trousers, work shirts, visored caps and brown boots. Their faces were dark and smudgy. 'Want to hear about the Silver Star I almost won?' Norman Bowker whispered, but none of the workmen looked up. Later they would blow colour into the sky. The lake would sparkle with reds and blues and greens, like a mirror, and the picnickers would make low sounds of appreciation.

'Well, see, it never stopped raining,' he would've said. 'The muck was everywhere, you couldn't get away from it.'

He would have paused a second.

Then he would have told about the night they bivouacked in a field along the Song Tra Bong. A big swampy field beside the river. There was a *ville* nearby, fifty metres downstream, and right away a dozen old *mama-sans* ran out and started yelling. A weird scene, he would've said. The *mama-sans* just stood there in the rain, soaking wet, yapping away about how this field was bad news. Number Ten, they said. Evil ground. Not a nice spot for nice GIs. Finally Lieutenant Cross had to exercise eminent domain. He got out his .45 and fired off a few rounds just to shoo them away. By then it was almost dark. So they set up a perimeter, ate chow, then crawled under their ponchos and tried to settle in for the night.

But the rain kept getting worse. And by midnight the field turned into soup.

'Just this deep, oozy soup,' he would've said. 'Like sewage or something. Thick and mushy. You couldn't sleep. You couldn't even lie down, not for long, because you'd start to sink under the soup. Real clammy. You could feel the crud coming up inside your boots and pants.'

Here, Norman Bowker would have squinted against the low sun. He would have kept his voice cool, no self-pity. 'But the worst part,' he would've said quietly, 'was the smell. Partly it was the river—a dead fish smell—but it was something else, too. Finally somebody figured it out. What this was, it was a shit field. The village toilet. No indoor plumbing, right? So they used the field. I mean, we were camped in a goddamn *shit* field.'

He imagined Sally Kramer closing her eyes.

If she were with him, in the car, she would've said, 'Stop it. I don't like that word.'

'That's what it *was*.'

'All right, but you don't have to use that word.'

'Fine. What should we call it?'

She would would have glared at him. 'I don't know. Just stop it.'

Clearly, he thought, this was not a story for Sally Kramer. She was Sally Gustafson now. No doubt Max would've liked it, the irony in particular, but Max had become a pure idea, which was its own irony. It was just too bad. If his father were here, riding shotgun around the lake, the old man might have glanced over for a second, understanding perfectly well that it was not a question of offensive language but of fact. His father would have sighed and folded his arms and waited.

'A shit field,' Norman Bowker would have said. 'And later that night I could've won the Silver Star for valour.'

'Right,' his father would've murmured, 'I hear you.'

The Chevy rolled smoothly across a viaduct and up the narrow tar road. To the right was open lake. To the left, across the road, most of the lawns were scorched dry like October corn. Hopelessly, round and round, a rotating sprinkler scattered lake water on Dr Mason's vegetable garden. Already the prairie had been baked dry, but in August it would get worse. The lake would turn green with bacteria, and the golf course would burn up, and the dragon-flies would crack open for want of good water.

The big Chevy curved past Centennial Beach and the A&W root beer stand.

It was his eighth revolution around the lake.

He followed the road past the handsome houses with their docks and wooden shingles. Back to Slater Park, across the causeway, around to Sunset Park, as though riding on tracks.

The two little boys were still trudging along on their seven-mile hike.

Out on the lake, the man in the stalled motorboat still fiddled with his engine. The pair of mud hens floated like wooden decoys, and the water-skiers looked tanned and athletic, and the high school band was packing up its instruments, and the woman in the pedal-pushers patiently rebaited her hook for one last try.

Quaint, he thought.

A hot summer day and it was all very quaint and remote. The four workmen had nearly completed their preparations for the evening fireworks.

F acing the sun again, Norman Bowker decided it was nearly seven o'clock. Not much later the tired radio announcer confirmed it, his voice rocking itself into a deep Sunday snooze. If Max Arnold were here, he would say something about the announcer's fatigue, and relate it to the bright pink in the sky, and the war, and courage. A pity that Max was gone. And a pity about his father, who had his own war and who now preferred silence.

Still, there was so much to say.

How the rain never stopped. How the cold worked into your bones. Sometimes the bravest thing on earth was to sit through the night and feel the cold in your bones. Courage was not always a matter of yes or no. Sometimes it came in degrees, like the cold; sometimes you were very brave up to a point and then beyond that point you were not so brave. In certain situations you could do incredible things, you could advance towards enemy fire, but in other situations, which were not nearly so bad, you had trouble keeping your eyes open. Sometimes, like the night in the shit field, the difference between courage and cowardice was something small and stupid.

The way the earth bubbled. And the smell.

In a soft voice, without flourishes, he would have told the exact truth.

'Late in the night,' he would've said, 'we took some mortar fire.'

He would've explained how it was still raining, and how the clouds were pasted to the field, and how the mortar rounds seemed to come right out of the clouds. Everything was black and wet. The field just exploded. Rain and slop and shrapnel, nowhere to run, and all they could do was worm down into slime and cover up and wait. He would've described the crazy things he saw. Weird things. Like how at one point he noticed a guy lying next to him in the sludge, completely buried except for his face, and how after a moment the guy rolled his eyes and winked at him. The noise was fierce. Heavy thunder, and mortar rounds, and people yelling. Some of the men began shooting up flares. Red and green and silver flares, all colours, and the rain came down in Technicolor.

The field was boiling. The shells made deep slushy craters, opening up all those years of waste, centuries' worth, and the smell came bubbling out of the earth. Two rounds hit close by. Then a third, even closer, and immediately, off to his left, he heard somebody screaming. It was Kiowa—he knew that. The sound was ragged and clotted up, but even so he knew the voice.

Rolling sideways, he crawled towards the screaming in the dark. The rain was hard and steady. Along the perimeter there were quick bursts of gunfire. Another round hit nearby, spraying up shit and water, and for a few moments he ducked down beneath the slime. He heard the valves in his heart. He heard the quick, feathering action of the hinges. Extraordinary, he thought. As he came up, a pair of red flares puffed open, a soft fuzzy glow, and in the glow he saw Kiowa's wide-open eyes settling down into the scum. Briefly, all he could do was watch. He heard himself moan. Then he moved again, crabbing forward, but when he got there Kiowa was almost completely under. There was a knee. There was an arm and a gold wrist-watch and part of a boot.

He could not describe what happened next, not ever, but he would've tried. He would've spoken carefully so as to make it real for anyone who would listen.

There were bubbles where Kiowa's head should've been.

His left hand was curled open; the finger-nails were filthy; the wrist-watch gave off a green phosphorescent shine as it slipped beneath the muck.

He would've talked about this, and how he grabbed Kiowa by the boot and tried to pull him out. He pulled hard but Kiowa was gone, and then suddenly he felt himself going too. He could taste it. It was in his nose and eyes. There were flares and mortar rounds, and the stink was everywhere—it was inside him, in his lungs—and he could no longer tolerate it. Not here, he thought. Not like this. He released Kiowa's boot and watched it slide away. Slowly, working his way up, he hoisted himself out of the deep mud, and then he lay still and tasted the shit in his mouth and closed his eyes and listened to the rain and explosions and bubbling sounds.

He was alone.

He had lost his weapon but it did not matter. All he wanted was a bath.

Nothing else. A hot soapy bath.

Circling the lake, Norman Bowker remembered how his friend Kiowa had disappeared under the waste and water. 'I didn't flip out,' he would've said. 'I was cool. If things had gone right, if it hadn't been for that smell, I could've won the Silver Star.'

A good war story, he thought, but it was not a war for war stories, nor talk of valour, and nobody in town wanted to know about the terrible stink. They wanted good intentions and good deeds. But the town was not to blame, really. It was actually quite a nice little town, very clean, and people had no need for shit fields.

Norman Bowker lit a cigarette and cranked open his window. Seven thirty-five, he decided.

The lake had divided into two halves. One half still glistened, the other was caught in shadow. Along the causeway, the two little boys marched on. The man in the stalled motorboat yanked frantically on the cord to his engine, and the two mud hens sought supper at the bottom of the lake, tails bobbing. He passed Sunset Park once again, and more houses, and the junior college and the tennis courts, and the picnickers, who now sat waiting for the evening fireworks. The high school band was gone. The woman in pedal-pushers patiently reeled in her line.

Although it was not yet dusk, the A&W was already awash in neon lights.

He manoeuvred his father's Chevy into one of the parking slots, let the engine idle, and sat back. The place was doing a good holiday business. Mostly kids, it seemed, and a few farmers in for the day. He did not recognize any of the faces. A slim, hipless young carhop passed by, but when he hit the horn, she did not seem to notice. Her eyes slid sideways. She hooked a tray to the window of a Firebird, laughing lightly, leaning forward to chat with the three boys inside.

He felt invisible in the soft twilight. Straight ahead, over the take-out counter, swarms of mosquitoes electrocuted themselves against an aluminium Pest-Rid machine.

It was a calm, quiet summer evening.

He honked again, this time leaning on the horn. The young carhop turned slowly, as if puzzled, then said something to the boys in the Firebird and moved reluctantly towards him. Pinned to her shirt was a badge that said EAT MAMA BURGERS.

When she reached his window, she stood straight up so that all he could see was the badge.

'Mama Burger,' he said. 'Maybe some fries, too.'

The girl sighed, leaned down, and shook her head. Her eyes were as lovely and airy-light as cotton candy.

'You blind?' she said.

She put out her hand and tapped an intercom attached to a steel post.

'God, you *must* be blind. Punch the button and place your order. All I do is carry the dumb trays.'

She stared at him for a moment. Briefly, he thought, a question lingered in her fuzzy eyes, but then she turned and punched the button for him and returned to her friends in the Firebird.

The intercom squeaked and said, 'Order.'

'Mama Burger and fries,' Norman Bowker said.

'Affirmative, copy clear. No rootie-tootie?'

'Rootie-tootie?'

'You know, man—*root* beer.'

'A small one.'

'Roger-dodger. Repeat: one Mama, one fries, one small beer.

147

Fire for effect. Stand by.'

The intercom squeaked and went dead.

'Out,' said Norman Bowker.

When the girl brought his tray, he ate quickly, without looking up. The tired radio announcer in Des Moines gave the time, almost eight-thirty. Dark was pressing in tight now, and he wished there were somewhere to go. In the morning he'd check out some job possibilities. Shoot a few buckets down at the Y, maybe wash the Chevy.

He finished his root beer and pushed the intercom button.

'Order,' said the tinny voice.

'All done.'

'That's *it*?'

'I guess so.'

'Hey, loosen up,' the voice said. 'What you really need, friend?'

Norman Bowker smiled.

'Well,' he said, 'how'd you like to hear—'

He stopped and shook his head.

'Hear *what*, man?'

'Nothing.'

'Well, hey,' the intercom said, 'I'm sure as fuck not *going* anywhere. Screwed to a post, for Christ sake. Go ahead, try me.'

'Nothing.'

'You sure?'

'Positive. All done.'

The intercom made a light sound of disappointment. 'Your choice, I guess. Over an' out.'

'Out,' said Norman Bowker.

On his tenth turn around the lake he passed the hiking boys for the last time. The man in the stalled motorboat was gone; the mud hens were gone. Beyond the lake, over Sally Gustafson's house, the sun had left a smudge of purple on the horizon. The band shell was deserted, and the woman in the pedal-pushers quietly reeled in her line, and Dr Mason's sprinkler went round and round.

On his eleventh revolution he switched off the air-conditioning, opened up his window, and rested his elbow comfortably on the sill, driving with one hand.

There was nothing to say. He could not talk about it and never would. The evening was smooth and warm. If it had been possible, which it wasn't, he would have explained how his friend Kiowa slipped away that night beneath the dark swampy field. He was folded in with the war; he was part of the waste. Turning on his headlights, driving slowly, Norman Bowker remembered how he had tried to save the guy. He had taken hold of Kiowa's boot and pulled hard, but then he'd felt himself being sucked under, and the smell was simply too much and he'd backed off and in that way he had lost the Silver Star. One of those sad things. He had tried, though, so it wasn't cowardice. It was gallantry, in fact, of the common sort. But he had not tried hard enough, nor could he make himself try again, and therefore he had lost his chance to win the Silver Star for uncommon valour.

He wished he could've explained some of this. How he had been braver than he ever thought possible, but how he had not been so brave as he wanted to be. The distinction was important. Max Arnold, who loved fine lines, would've appreciated it. And his father, who already knew, would've nodded.

'The truth,' Norman Bowker would've said, 'is I let the guy go.'

'Maybe he was already gone.'

'He wasn't.'

'But maybe.'

'No, I could feel it. He wasn't. Some things you can feel.'

His father would have been quiet for a while, watching the headlights against the narrow tar road.

'Well, anyway,' the old man would've said. 'There's still the seven medals.'

'I suppose.'

'Seven honeys.'

'Right.'

On his twelfth revolution, the sky went crazy with colour.

He pulled into Sunset Park and stopped in the shadow of a picnic shelter. After a time, he got out, walked down to the beach, and waded into the lake without undressing. The water felt warm against his skin. He put his head under. He opened his lips, very slightly, for the taste, then he stood up and folded his arms and watched the fireworks. For a small town, he decided, it was a pretty good show.

Notes

'Speaking of Courage' was written, in 1975, at the suggestion of Norman Bowker, who three years later hanged himself in the locker room of a YMCA in his home town in central Iowa.

In the spring of 1975, near the time of Saigon's final collapse, I received a long, disjointed letter in which Bowker described the problem of finding a meaningful use for his life after the war. He had worked briefly as an automotive parts salesman, a janitor, a car wash attendant and a short-order cook at the local A&W fast food franchise. None of these jobs, he said, had lasted more than ten weeks. He lived with his parents, who supported him and who treated him with kindness and obvious love. At one point he had enrolled in the junior college in his home town, but the course work, he said, seemed too abstract, too distant, with nothing real or tangible at stake, certainly not the stakes of a war. He dropped out after eight months. He spent his mornings in bed. In the afternoons he played pickup basketball at the Y, and then at night he drove around town in his father's car, mostly alone, or with a six-pack of beer, cruising.

'The thing is,' he wrote, 'there's no place to go. Not just in this lousy little town. In general. My life, I mean. It's almost like I got killed over in Nam . . . Hard to describe. That night when Kiowa got wasted, I sort of sank down into the sewage with him . . . feels like I'm still in deep shit.'

The letter covered seventeen handwritten pages, jumping from self-pity to anger to irony to guilt to a kind of feigned indifference. He didn't know what to feel. In the middle of the letter, for example, he reproached himself for complaining too much:

> God, this is starting to sound like some jerkoff vet crying in his beer. Sorry about that. I'm no basket case—not even any bad dreams. And I don't feel like anybody mistreats me or anything, except sometimes people act

too nice, too polite, like they're afraid they might ask the wrong question . . . But I shouldn't bitch. One thing I hate—really hate—is all those whiner-vets. Guys snivelling about how they didn't get any parades. Such absolute crap. I mean, who in his right mind wants a *parade*? Or getting his back clapped by a bunch of patriotic idiots who don't know jack about what it feels like to kill people or get shot at or sleep in the rain or watch your buddy go down underneath the mud? Who *needs* it?

Anyhow, I'm basically A-OK. Home free!! So why not come down for a visit sometime and we'll chase pussy and shoot the breeze and tell each other old war lies. A good long bull session, you know?

I felt it coming, and near the end of the letter it came. He explained that he had read my first book, *If I Die in a Combat Zone*, which he liked except for the 'bleeding-heart political parts'. For half a page he talked about how much the book had meant to him, how it brought back all kinds of memories, the *villes* and paddies and rivers, and how he recognized most of the characters, including himself, even though almost all of the names were changed.

Then Bowker came straight out with it:

What you should do, Tim, is write a story about a guy who feels like he got zapped over in that shithole. A guy who can't get his act together and just drives around town all day and can't think of any damn place to go and doesn't know how to get there anyway. This guy wants to talk about it, but he *can't* . . . If you want, you can use the stuff in this letter. (But not my real name, OK?) I'd write it myself except I can't ever find any words, if you know what I mean, and I can't figure out what exactly to *say*. Something about the field that night. The way Kiowa just disappeared into the crud. You were there, Tim—you can tell it.

Norman Bowker's letter hit me hard. For years I'd felt a certain smugness about how easily I had made the shift from war to peace, a nice smooth glide—no flashbacks or midnight sweats. The war was over, after all. And the thing to do was go on. So I took pride in sliding gracefully from Vietnam to graduate school, from Chu Lai to Harvard, from one world to another. In ordinary conversation I never spoke much about the war, certainly not in detail, and yet ever since my return I had been talking about it virtually non-stop through my writing. Telling stories seemed a natural, inevitable process, like clearing the throat. Partly catharsis; partly communication, it was a way of grabbing people by the shirt and explaining exactly what had happened to me, how I'd allowed myself to get dragged into a wrong war, all the mistakes I'd made, all the terrible things I had seen and done.

I did not look on my work as therapy, and still don't. Yet when I received Norman Bowker's letter, it occurred to me that my writing had led me through a swirl of memories that might otherwise have ended in paralysis or worse. By telling stories, you objectify your own experience. You separate it from yourself. You pin down certain truths. You make up others. You start sometimes with an incident that truly happened, like that night in the shit field, and you carry it forward by inventing incidents which did not in fact occur but which none the less help to clarify and explain.

In any case, Norman Bowker's letter had an effect. It haunted me for more than a month, not the words so much as its desperation, and I resolved finally to take him up on his story suggestion. At the time I was at work on a new novel, *Going After Cacciato*, and one summer morning I sat down and began a chapter titled 'Speaking of Courage'. The emotional core came directly from Bowker's letter: the simple need to talk. To provide a dramatic frame, I collapsed events into a single time and place, a car circling a lake on a quiet afternoon in mid-summer, using the lake as a nucleus around which the story would orbit. As he'd requested, I did not use Norman Bowker's name, instead substituting the name of my novel's main character, Paul Berlin. For the scenery I borrowed heavily from my own home town. Wholesale thievery, in fact. I lifted up Worthington, Minnesota—the lake, the road, the causeway, the woman in pedal-pushers, the junior college, the handsome houses and docks and boats and public parks—and carried it all a few hundred miles south and transplanted it on the Iowa prairie. The writing went quickly and easily. I drafted the piece in a week or two, fiddled with it for another week, then published it as a separate short story.

Almost immediately, though, I felt a sense of failure. The details of Norman Bowker's story were missing. In this original version, which I still conceived as part of the novel, I had been forced to omit the shit field and the rain and the death of Kiowa, replacing this material with events that better fit the book's narrative. As a consequence I'd lost the natural counterpoint between the lake and the field. A metaphoric unity was broken. What the piece needed, and did not have, was the terrible killing suction of that shit field.

As the novel developed over the next year, and as my own ideas clarified, it became apparent that the chapter had no proper home in the larger narrative. *Going After Cacciato* was a war story; 'Speaking of Courage' was a post-war story. Two different time periods, two different sets of issues. There was no choice but to remove the piece entirely. The mistake, in part, had been in trying to wedge the piece into a novel. Beyond that, though, something about the story had frightened me—I was afraid to speak directly, afraid to remember—and in the end the piece had been ruined by a failure to tell the full and exact truth about our night in the shit field.

Over the next several months, as it often happens, I managed to erase the story's flaws from my memory, taking pride in a shadowy, idealized recollection of its virtues. When the piece appeared in an anthology of short fiction, I sent a copy off to Norman Bowker with the thought that it might please him. His reaction was short and somewhat bitter.

'It's not terrible,' he wrote me, 'but you left out Vietnam. Where's Kiowa? Where's all the shit?'

Eight months later he hanged himself.

In August of 1978, after I'd mailed several letters without a response, his mother sent me a brief note in which she explained what had happened. He'd been playing pickup basketball at the Y; after two hours he went off for a drink of water; he used a jump rope; his friends found him hanging from a water-pipe. There was no suicide note, no message of any kind. 'Norman was a quiet boy,' his mother wrote, 'and I don't suppose he wanted to bother anybody.'

N ow, a decade after his death, I'm hoping that 'Speaking of Courage' makes good on Norman Bowker's silence. And I hope it's a better story. Although the old structure remains, the piece has been radically revised, in some places by severe cutting, in other places by the addition of new material. Norman is back in the story, where he belongs, and I doubt he would mind that his real name appears. The central incident—our long night in the shit field along the Song Tra Bong—has been restored to the piece. It was hard stuff to write. Kiowa, after all, had been a close friend, and for years I've avoided talking about his death and my own complicity in it. Even here it's not easy. In the interests of truth, however, I want to make it clear that Norman Bowker was in no way responsible for what happened to Kiowa. Norman did not experience a failure of nerve that night. He did not freeze up or lose the Silver Star for valour. That part of the story is my own.

PATRICK MCGRATH

A CHILDHOOD IN

BROADMOOR

HOSPITAL

In 1856 the Lunacy Commissioners announced that an asylum capable of accommodating 600 criminal lunatics was to be built in the Berkshire countryside, and that Sir Joshua Jebb, the architect of Pentonville and Holloway prisons, was to build it: thus was Broadmoor born. Ninety-nine years later my father was appointed its tenth medical superintendent.

When I went to the hospital as a boy, to see my father, I would be met by a male nurse in a black uniform with a peaked cap and a bunch of large keys attached to his trouser pocket. He led me through a double-locked door, along a flagstoned corridor, through a barred gate and down a cloister. We then crossed a courtyard, and, after a second double-locked door, entered my father's office. A huge room this, with a huge desk, and beside the desk windows with a view over broad terraces and sports fields sweeping down to the perimeter wall. Beyond the wall there was farm land, gradually giving way to the wooded hills of Hampshire. What I remember most vividly about this room is a water-colour of a Victorian seaman. He is bent slightly at the waist, lifting his hat with one hand and clutching a fiddle and bow with the other. His left leg also is lifted, only there is no left leg; sticking out of his bell-bottoms is a wooden stump.

'Sailor' was painted by Richard Dadd, the Victorian artist who stabbed his father to death in Chobham in 1843, apparently believing him to be the devil, and then fled to France on a mission to kill the Pope. He was captured after attempting to cut a man's throat in a coach and was eventually confined to the dark, cramped criminal wing of Bethlem Hospital, where he remained for twenty years until being transferred to Broadmoor. There, in tranquil, spacious surroundings, he resumed his painting, controlled, so he thought, by the Egyptian god Osiris. He died of consumption in the hospital in 1886, and is buried not far from the house I grew up in.

That house, the superintendent's house, also built by Joshua Jebb with the same red brick as Broadmoor, is a hundred yards from the main gate: Kentigern, my parents named it, after the patron saint of Glasgow—a big, draughty house complete with outhouses, scullery and servants' quarters, though by 1955, when we arrived, the servants were long gone. Granny lived up there instead.

Every Sunday morning I went with my family—my parents, my brothers Simon and Stephen, my sister Judy and Granny—to the chapel for Mass, and from a side-aisle watched the men come shuffling in wearing the baggy flannel trousers and ill-fitting jackets made in the hospital tailor's shop; their shoes squeaked. The patients I knew best were the men in the working party that looked after the garden. They always wore stout work boots, yellow corduroy trousers and black donkey jackets with plastic strips across the shoulders. The best time of the day was smoko, when they had their tea. My mother came out of the back door of Kentigern with a large brown tray with teapot, mugs and biscuits on it, and cried: 'Smoko!' The cry was taken up, passed from mouth to mouth until it was heard in the furthest reaches of the garden, and the men came tramping up towards the house, corduroys flapping, and settled down on wooden boxes and old chairs in the barnlike garage behind the house. There they drank their tea and smoked their roll-ups and kicked a plastic football around the yard. Joe Artless (Mr Artless to me) was the nurse in charge of the working party, and when the time came he knocked the ashes out of his pipe and rose to his feet, and the men went back to work.

These were the friends of my early boyhood, men who twenty years earlier would still have been called 'criminal lunatics'. The first I met was Frank, who built me a swing that hung from an iron bar that he made in the hospital workshop and set high between a pair of tall pines. I treated Frank as an uncle, following him around while he went about his work, chattering away. In the autumn, when he filled his wheelbarrow with dead leaves he would let me ride on top of the heap, clutching a garden fork and shrieking like a little sea god in his chariot. I once asked Frank what he had 'done', and he shook his head and told me, kindly, sadly, that it was 'very bad'—but said no more.

Many of the patients had committed acts of violence, often in a richly bizarre manner, involving amputation, evisceration or other forms of disfigurement. Kitchen knives and garden utensils seemed to have been most often employed. One man's project was to liberate the souls of virgins, believing that having ascended to heaven they would then return to redeem and purify him. To this end he murdered a number of women with a hammer. Another man was charged with nothing more than stealing a hoe. But he wanted the hoe to kill his father, and he wanted to kill his father to get him out of the way, for with his father out of the way he could do what he really wanted to do, which was kill his mother, a case of what my father called 'inverted, unresolved Oedipus'.

My father has known all the interesting English murderers since the war. The most disturbed men were housed in Block Six. Even now the words 'Block Six' sound sinister to me, perhaps because I never entered the building and remember, rather, the way the small boys on the Broadmoor estate always talked of it. Once at dusk, when I was crossing a yard inside the hospital with my father, a terrible scream suddenly came from one of the high windows of Block Six, a scream charged with the utmost misery. Startled, I looked up at my father. 'Poor John,' he murmured, and by his tone I understood that *he* understood why poor John screamed; and the fact that he understood it robbed the scream of its terror for me.

Block Six has since been renamed. It is now called Monmouth House.

In the woods behind the Broadmoor Cemetery, where Richard Dadd is buried, there is a slender metal tower with a siren at the top. Its function is to warn the countryside that an escape has taken place. Every Monday morning at exactly ten o'clock it was tested, its awful sing-song drone wailing out across our sleepy corner of Berkshire like the funeral lament of some bereaved giant. For my father that wail was a terrible sound; an escape brought the press and the politicians down upon him, besides which the local people were endangered. I remember Frank Mitchell, a member of the Kray gang, going over the wall. He was a resident of Block Six, and during his escape he terrorized with an axe a family in Wokingham, a market town five miles away.

His escape was classic. Somehow he got hold of a hack-saw and one night sawed through the bars of his room. He made his way along a ledge and over an internal wall, then across a yard to the perimeter wall, where he had spotted a point at which it could be scaled. Over he went, and away. I was seven at the time, and I remember the policemen and the dogs, the urgency and high seriousness at home. Soldiers arrived but my father insisted that they be disarmed before they joined the search-parties. I was attending Broadmoor Primary School, and for the next few days we walked down the hill in groups accompanied by an adult. One morning I found a footprint in the mud at the foot of the wall and thrilled to the realization that I'd discovered where Mitchell had gone over; no one believed me. When he was recaptured some days later I was among the throng of Broadmoor folk who lined the road to the main gate to watch the Black Maria and the 'mad axeman' go by. He was transferred to Dartmoor Prison shortly afterwards, escaped from there in 1966, and was subsequently murdered by the gang that had helped him to get out. I am told on good authority that he is encased in a concrete pillar supporting a bridge over an East London motorway.

Christmas morning in Broadmoor began with my father making a morning tour of the male wards, a job he hated, for he felt like the governor of a workhouse, telling his chaps to eat up their Christmas pud. Some of the men appreciated the visit, but others turned away. It was not thought proper that my mother and the children should see those wards, so we met my father in the female wing, and as a family we made our tour there. The wards were decorated, and there were cakes and biscuits, but I hated those mornings. The women gushed and fussed and simpered about us, and I think now that we must have reminded them of their own children, whose destruction, in not a few cases, had brought them to Broadmoor in the first place. When my mother said she would have to discontinue these visits—she could never get back in time to prepare her Christmas dinner—the hospital kitchens responded by cooking her meal for her, and thereafter, at the end of the morning, we would find turkey and trimmings being borne, steaming, from the Broadmoor kitchens to the boot of the car, and thence back to Kentigern.

Later, in the afternoon, we had tea with the chaplain, a vast, Falstaffian character called Basil James, who could hit a cricket ball clear over the wall but was so fat he required a man to run between the wickets for him. My father remembers the Reverend

James pondering his memories of World War One, sadly recounting how, while laying telephone lines in no-man's-land, he had to kill a German soldier with a telephone head-set.

When we arrived at Broadmoor in 1955 the buildings were obsolete and overcrowded, with men sleeping in corridors and day-rooms. It was, in effect, a prison, and my father took upon himself the task of turning this prison into a hospital. I remember him coming home from work with a face black with tension, and I kept out of his path till he'd had a Scotch or two. He faced resistance not only from an old guard within Broadmoor but from his political masters in Whitehall also.

After I went away to school my links to Broadmoor weakened considerably, and it wasn't until 1973, when I spent several weeks actually working in the hospital, that I got to know the place again. My father, now in his fifties, had grown a beard and smoked cigars, and looked magisterially psychiatric.

Broadmoor had changed. There were now departments of clinical psychology and social work; there was a full complement of consultant psychiatrists; the attendants had been transformed into trained psychiatric nurses. There were also new problems, fierce interdisciplinary squabbles, for the air was thick with vigorous new paradigms, spawned variously of behaviourism, the human potential movement and the anti-psychiatry of Laing and Cooper. 'Not all consultants,' wrote my father in an annual report, 'found it easy to adjust their perceived independence, and statutory authority as responsible medical officers, to the constraints of the multidisciplinary approach.' What I saw during those few weeks was a stocky dynamic man, briskly decisive, at the height of his powers, indisputably in control of the institution he had been running for as long as anyone could remember.

Two years ago I returned to Kentigern with my brothers. Nobody lives there now; the house has become an office building. That wild garden is now very clipped; the hedges have disappeared; the stands of rhododendrons have been replaced by flat lawns. The garage, site of a thousand smokos—people park their cars there now.

Cautiously we entered. Inside we found that those huge

rooms, impossible to heat, where the families of Victorian superintendents could properly take their ease, no longer existed: the ceilings had been lowered and the rooms themselves had been partitioned into work stations, each with its typewriter and filing cabinet. Slowly we moved through the house; we could imagine superintendents past—Meyer, Orange, Hopwood—murmuring elegies, wringing their hands. My brother Simon, the youngest, was in tears: the room in which he had been born was now used to store stationery. The servants' wing, Granny's domain, was a lunch room with a hot-plate and an automatic coffee-maker.

I have in front of me a page from an old *Daily Express* with the banner headline: BEDLAM '68. The story describes in detail the overcrowding of the hospital, the problems this posed to security and the negative effects on staff morale. There's a photograph of my father and another of the main gate, with the caption: 'Broadmoor Hospital—home of 188 murderers'. The sub-head reads: 'Where 700 men live a nightmare.' I remember once going through a drawer in my father's study that I wasn't supposed to go through and finding a *News of the World* with two photographs on the front page, one of my father, one of a patient, with the headline: WHAT FOOL LET OUT THIS FIEND? But there was no caption to tell the reader who was the fool and who was the fiend.

My father recently told me about a woman in the female wing who, one night, under her bedclothes, noiselessly enucleated herself—took out her eyes—with a teaspoon. We had been talking about the schizophrenic's ability to pervert bodily sensation in the service of some dominant delusional theme. This woman felt no pain and was found the next morning among her bloody bedclothes wide-awake. I had instigated the conversation; at the time I was trying to render schizophrenic experience in a novel. My father would have liked me to become a doctor, but what growing up in Broadmoor gave me, that glimpse of the limits to which men and women can be driven by psychotic illness, has stimulated, instead, the writing of fiction. Not that I could have followed in my father's footsteps anyway, for his job, after he retired, was chopped up into little pieces and divided among administrators and clinical directors: he was the last of the medical superintendents.

MORE FACT THAN FICTION

20/20
MAGAZINE

ENTERTAINMENT, THE ARTS & MUCH MORE. NOVEMBER 1989. No.8. £1.50.

20/20

THE *20/20* INTERVIEW
DE NIRO

MONTHLY
£1.50

PAUL THEROUX
FIRST TRAIN
JOURNEY

I had been travelling for more than ten years—in Europe, Asia and Africa—and it had not occurred to me to write a travel book. I had always somewhat disliked travel books: they seemed self-indulgent, unfunny and rather selective. I had an idea that the travel writer left a great deal out of his books and put the wrong things in. I hated sight-seeing, yet sight-seeing constituted much of the travel writer's material: the pyramids, the Taj Mahal, the Vatican, the paintings here, the mosaics there. In an age of mass tourism, everyone set off to see the same things, and that was what travel writing seemed to be about. I am speaking of the early 1970s.

The travel book was a bore. A bore wrote it and bores read it. It annoyed me that a traveller would suppress the moments of desperation or fear or lust, the details of meals, the names of books read to kill time, the condition of toilets. I had done enough travelling to know that half of it was delay or nuisance—buses breaking down and hotel clerks being rude and market traders being rapacious. The truth of travel was interesting and off-key, and few people ever wrote about it.

Now and then one would read the truth: Evelyn Waugh being mistaken for his brother Alec in *Labels*; or Naipaul's good intentions and bad temper in parts of *An Area of Darkness*; or in a fragment like the following from Anthony Trollope's *The West Indies and the Spanish Main*:

> I was in a shoemaker's shop at St Thomas [Jamaica], buying a pair of boots, when a negro entered quickly and in a loud voice said he wanted a pair of pumps. He was a labouring man fresh from his labour. He had on an old hat—what in Ireland men would call a caubeen; he was in his shirt-sleeves, and was barefooted. As the only shopman was looking for my boots, he was not attended to at the moment.
>
> 'Want a pair of pumps—directerly,' he roared out in a very dictatorial voice.
>
> 'Sit down for a moment,' said the shopman, 'and I will attend to you.'
>
> He did sit down, but did so in the oddest fashion. He dropped himself suddenly into a chair, and at the same

moment rapidly raised his legs from the ground; and as he did so fastened his hands across them just below his knees, so as to keep his feet suspended from his arms. This he contrived to do in such a manner that the moment his body reached the chair his feet left the ground. I looked on in amazement, thinking he was mad.

'Give I a bit of carpet,' he screamed out; still holding up his feet, but with much difficulty.

'Yes, yes,' said the shopman, still searching for the boots.

'Give I a bit of carpet directerly,' he again exclaimed. The seat of the chair was very narrow, and the back was straight, and the position was not easy, as my reader will ascertain if he attempt it. He was half-choked with anger and discomfort.

The shopman gave him the bit of carpet. Most men and women will remember that such bits of carpet are common in shoemakers' shops. They are supplied, I believe, in order that they who are delicate should not soil their stockings on the floor.

The gentleman in search of the pumps had seen that people of dignity were supplied with such luxuries, and resolved to have his value for his money; but as he had on neither shoes nor stockings, the little bit of carpet was hardly necessary for his material comfort.

Something human had happened, and Trollope recorded it: that, it seemed to me, was the essence of good travel writing.

A traveller's itinerary was important too. Many travel books seemed to be accounts of a traveller becoming a resident. This was not travel at all, but rather a kind of extended visit that I knew well from having lived in Malawi and Uganda and Singapore. I had settled down in those places, I was working, I had a driver's licence, I went shopping every Saturday. It had never occurred to me to write a travel book about any of it. Travel had to do with movement and truth: with trying everything, offering yourself to experience and then reporting it.

Choosing the best route, the correct mode of travel, was the surest way, I felt, of gaining the experience that would lead to writing. It had to be total immersion, a deliberate trip through the hinterland rather than flying from one big city to another, which didn't seem to me to be travel at all. The travel books I liked were off-beat in some way—Trollope's and Naipaul's, Henry Miller's *The Air-Conditioned Nightmare* (America, coast to coast, by car), Mark Twain's *Following The Equator* (a lecture-tour around the world).

My speculations on travel writing took place in the autumn of 1972, when I was teaching for a semester at the University of Virginia. I was working on one novel, and awaiting the publication of another. In those days I began a new book as soon as I finished the one I was working on. My wife was in London with our two children, and she was working—indeed, earning a good living—but I still felt I was the bread-winner and that I was not earning enough. My fee for the new book was 250 pounds, and I assumed I would not get much more for the book I was writing. Money is a clumsy subject, but money was crucial in my decision to write my first travel book—simply, I needed it. When I mentioned the possibility of such a book to my American editor, she was delighted. She said, 'We'll give you an advance.' I had never before received an advance. Normally, I wrote a book and submitted it and was paid; I had never been given money for an unwritten book.

It is often the case that you begin to think clearly about your intentions when someone asks you very specific questions. I intended my travel book to be a series of long train journeys, but I had no idea where I wanted to go. I saw a book with lots of people and lots of dialogue and no sight-seeing. My editor's questioning made me think hard about it, and I thought: *Trains through Asia*. I was determined to start in London, and to take the Orient Express. My route would take me through Turkey, into Iran, into Baluchistan, and after a short bus ride I could catch a train in Zahedan, go into Pakistan and more or less chug through the rest of Asia—to Hanoi, through China, Mongolia and the Soviet Union. Much of this, on closer examination, proved impractical or impossible. The Chinese Embassy in 1972 simply hung up when I said I wanted a visa to take trains through China. I had to wait fourteen years before I was able to take that trip.

There was a war in Baluchistan—I rerouted myself through Afghanistan. I decided to include Japan and the whole of the Trans-Siberian. I didn't mind where I went as long as it was in Asia and had a railway system and visas were available. I saw myself puffing along from country to country, simply changing trains.

Meanwhile I was finishing my novel. It was about rural England and was rather ghostly and solemn. I wanted my next to be a sunny book. I had just about decided on my travel itinerary when I delivered my novel to my British publisher. He suggested we have lunch. Almost before we had started eating he told me he disliked it. 'It will hurt your reputation,' was how he put it. 'But I want to publish your travel book.' I had told him I had signed a contract for this with my American publisher. I said that if he published my novel he could have the travel book. 'If you twist my arm I'll publish your novel,' he said.

I found a new publisher in Britain. I had greater reason than ever for publishing the travel book: I doubted my ability to earn a living writing fiction.

I think of the circumstances surrounding *The Great Railway Bazaar* rather than the trip itself. I hated leaving my family behind in London. I had never taken such a trip, I felt encumbered by an advance on royalties—modest though it was; most of my writer friends mocked the idea.

I never got around to worrying about the trip itself. I was beset by an obscure ache that was both mental and physical—the lingering anxiety that I was going to die. I had always had the idea that my particular exit would be made via an appointment in Samarra, and that I would go a great distance and endure enormous discomfort in order to meet my death. If I chose to sit at home and eat and drink it would never occur. I imagined it would be a silly accident, like what happened to the monk and mystic Thomas Merton: he left his monastery in Kentucky after twenty-five years and accidentally electrocuted himself on the frayed wires of a fan in Bangkok a week later.

I left London on 19 September 1973. It was a grey day. I had a bad cold. My wife waved me goodbye. Almost immediately I felt I had made an absurd mistake. I hadn't the slightest idea of what I was doing. I became very gloomy and to cheer myself up and give myself the illusion that this was work I began to take voluminous notes. From the time I left until the moment I arrived back in England four months later I filled one notebook after another. I wrote everything down—conversations, descriptions of people and places, details of trains, trivia, even criticism of the novels I happened to be reading. I still have some of those books, and on the blank back pages of Joyce's *Exiles*, Chekhov's stories and Endo's *Silence*, I have scribbled small insectile notes, which I amplified when I transferred them to my large notebooks. I always wrote in the past tense.

The trip recorded is the trip I took. I changed the names of people I wished to protect, but many names I left. I had found a structure for the book in a series of train journeys, and I simply plunged in. I had never read a book quite like the one I was writing. This worried me as well as made me hopeful. The writing of the book took the same amount of time as the trip itself, four months.

That was almost fifteen years ago. *The Great Railway Bazaar* is still in print and sells well. Some people think it is the only book I have ever written, which annoys me. I have written other books that are more fluent and informative. For example, I mention in *The Great Railway Bazaar* that my train passed through Niš in Yugoslavia. But I never bothered to find out anything about Niš. I have just read that it was the birthplace of the Emperor Constantine. The *Blue Guide* continues: 'Though not a pleasant place in itself, Niš has several interesting monuments.' I now realize why I did not linger in Niš.

I did not know when I wrote my *Railway Bazaar* (I got the title from a street-name in India) that every journey is unique. My book is about my trip, not yours or anyone else's. If someone had come with me and written a book about the trip, it would have been a different book from mine. I also did not know that every trip has a historical dimension. After I returned home political changes occurred in the countries I had travelled through. The Shah was deposed and Iran became very dangerous for the traveller;

Afghanistan went to war with itself; India and Pakistan restored their rail link. Laos shut its borders to foreigners and exiled its royalty. Vietnam repaired its railway, so that now it is possible to travel by train from Ho Chi Minh City (Saigon) to Hanoi. Many trains were taken out of service, most notably the Orient Express. The new train that plies from London to Venice under that name is for rich idle people who have selfish, sumptuous fantasies about travel that bear no relation to the real thing. However awful my old Orient Express was, at least it carried a range of passengers—rich and poor, old and young. It was cheap and friendly, and, like all great trains, it was a world on wheels.

When I wrote *The Great Railway Bazaar* I was groping in the dark—although I took care to disguise the fact. I may seem very self-assured in it, but it was simply my way of whistling to keep my spirits up. I knew that I had taken on a venerable genre, the travel book, and was writing it in my own way, to suit my peculiar trip and temperament. It was not like a novel: which requires inspiration and intense imagining and a long period alone in a room.

I began writing a novel soon after finishing my travel book. I got the idea for it in Vietnam and even mentioned it in *Railway Bazaar*: 'From the back of the train I could see market women and children reoccupying the track, and once—a swift sight of a leaping man—I thought I saw an American . . . If one were to write about Vietnam in any coherent way one would have to begin with these outsiders.'

A travel book, I had discovered, was a deliberate act—like the act of travel itself. It took health and strength and confidence. When I finished a novel I never knew whether I would be able to write another one. But I knew, when I finished my first travel book, that I would be able to do it again.

PATRICIA HIGHSMITH

SCENE OF

THE CRIME

Tom Ripley in my first book about him is a young man of
twenty-five, restless and jobless in New York, living
temporarily in a friend's apartment. He was orphaned early
and brought up by a rather stingy aunt in Boston. He has some
talent for mathematics and mimicry, and the two abilities enable
him to carry on a small game of scaring American tax-payers by
letter and telephone: he demands from them 'further payment' to
an Internal Revenue Service office whose branch, he says, is at a
certain address: it is the address of the friend with whom he is
staying, and Ripley takes the letters when they arrive, though he
can do nothing with the cheques inside them except chuckle with an
odd satisfaction.

When Ripley finds himself followed one evening in Manhattan
streets by a middle-aged man, his first thought is that the man is a
police agent, or could be, sent to apprehend him for his fraudulent
tax game. The follower turns out to be the father of an acquaintance
Ripley has trouble at first in remembering: Dickie Greenleaf, who
is now living in Europe, says the father.

Herbert Greenleaf invites Tom to dinner the next evening, and
here Tom meets Dickie's mother and has a glimpse of the finer
things of life: good furniture, silverware at the table, order and
politeness. These things, Tom realizes not for the first time, are his
aspirations. Furthermore, the Greenleafs offer to pay Tom's
expenses to Italy and back. Tom agrees to go.

It is Tom's first trip to Europe. He arrives in Dickie Greenleaf's
small village and looks him up. The longer he stays with Dickie the
more Tom envies the modest but steady income from a trust in
America, envies him his independence and what seems to Tom his
education in the ways of Europeans. But when Dickie catches Tom
trying on some of his clothes, Dickie loses his temper, and is on the
brink of asking Tom to get out of the house. But they go together to
San Remo, and Tom kills Dickie when they are alone in a small
motor boat at some distance from the shore. Tom sinks the body
with stones, scuttles the boat in the same manner. The next day he
returns to Dickie's villa, where he begins to invent stories about
Dickie's disappearance.

Tom is questioned about, but never accused of, Dickie's
murder. It is the only murder Tom deeply regrets and is ashamed of,

because he feels he did it out of selfishness, greed, envy, temper. For a while, he assumes Dickie's identity, takes his passport and uses it, writes a will in his own favour and signs Dickie's name to it. The father, Herbert Greenleaf, swallows all this. Tom Ripley is on his way, independent and determined to climb, to better himself— as he sees it.

I remember the place where Ripley was born, in the sense of being a story-less image in my memory. It is Positano, on my first trip there in 1951, late summer or early autumn. I was in a hotel with a friend, and our room or rooms had a balcony overlooking the beach and the sea. The shore there is a cosy curve with little fishing boats tied up or anchored. The beach is pebbly and disagreeable underfoot, however. One morning around six, I woke up and stepped out on to the terrace. All was cool and quiet, the cliffs rose high behind me and were out of sight then, but visible to right and left. Not a soul was around, nothing stirred except one or two gulls, then I noticed a solitary young man in shorts and sandals with a towel flung over his shoulder, making his way along the beach from right to left. He was looking downward—as who wouldn't, because of the stones and pebbles. I could just see that his hair was straight and darkish. There was an air of pensiveness about him, maybe unease. And why was he alone? He did not look like the athletic type who would take a cold swim alone at an early hour. Had he quarrelled with someone? What was on his mind? I never saw him again. I did not even write anything in my *cahier* about him. What would there have been to say? He looked like a thousand other American tourists in Europe that summer. I had the feeling that he was an American.

Months later, the beach scene returned to me. I had written short stories and a couple of articles in the meantime, no doubt. I was becoming better acquainted with Europe and the way people lived in France, Germany and Italy. It was my second trip to Europe, and it was to last two and a quarter years and include Trieste and Munich. I began to see not so much the attraction of Europe, but the possibility of an affinity with it, so deep and important that I might not wish or need to discuss it with friend or family. An idea came to me, of a young American drifter being sent to Europe to bring another American back home, if possible. I must have realized then that the idea resembled that of Henry James's *The Ambassadors*. However, mine was to have many a deviation from James's theme.

And then, when thinking the first Ripley book out, when writing the first pages, I am not sure that the Positano beach image with the solitary figure even came to my mind. The image was not on paper, I never used it in a Positano scene (I gave the town another name). It was like a faded yet indelible photograph in my mind, almost forgotten, until years later journalists asked me, 'Where did you get the idea for Ripley from?' and as I racked my mind to answer, to recall exactly *where*, the solitary figure on the beach returned to me, and I described his appearance—as I had seen it from two hundred metres or more. 'Did you ever meet this man?' would be the next question. No, and I am not sure that I ever saw him again in a Positano restaurant or bar. I had stayed in Positano a few days longer on that first trip, but it did not occur to me to look around for the American type I had seen that early morning. What good would it have done to see him? Close detail might even have spoiled everything. At any rate, when I had a chance of spotting this young man again, namely when I was in southern Italy, the idea for the first Ripley book was not in my mind.

I can imagine two reasons for criminals returning to the scene of their crime: to see if they have left any incriminating evidence, or to recapture the thrill or pleasure that doing the deed gave them maybe. A third reason, I suppose a credible one in some cases, is in order to be spotted, accused and captured. The annals of crime are full of examples of return, and murderers often admit to a desire to go back and linger at the spot, plainly to be apprehended and to receive attention.

The stretch of the Positano beach, which has not changed much except that it may now hold a few more boats or people, has no particular fascination for me. Ripley was not really born there, was just an image for me, and needed another element to spring to life: imagination, which came many months later.

JILL HARTLEY

POLAND

Warsaw.

Warsaw.

Warsaw.

Krakow.

Rock concert, Warsaw.

Orthodox pilgrims receiving blessing.

A man praying.

A pilgrim in an Orthodox churchyard.

Chapel of bones.

A street market.

SERPENTINE GALLERY

12 December - 28 January

Aleksandr Rodchenko
& Varvara Stepanova

Organised by the Third Eye Centre, Glasgow and New Beginnings in association with the Serpentine Gallery

Open 11.00am - 4.00pm   **ADMISSION FREE**

Recorded Information 01 723 9072
Underground : South Kensington Lancaster Gate
Buses : 9 10 12 52 88

KENSINGTON GARDENS LONDON W2 3XA

Josef Škvorecký

Feminine

Mystique

W e were sitting in the warehouse waiting for Kadeřábek. From the church on the square came the sound of the organ and the wailing of the old women:

Joyously we greeet thee,
Mother of Our Loooooord . . .

I tried to imagine Marie in her May dress, which was dark blue with a pattern of white flowers on it, and with a blue ribbon tied around her hair so that it cascaded down her back like a waterfall of gold. When she first showed up in school with her hair that way, Lexa told me a pony-tail was a phallic symbol. According to him, it meant that my chances with Marie, which had up till then been practically non-existent, were about to improve. But I hadn't yet read *Introductory Lectures on Psychoanalysis* (I was in line for it after Lexa, who'd borrowed it from someone's library) so I asked, naïvely, what a phallic symbol was. Lexa guffawed out loud, the teacher interpreted this as a deliberate disruption of his maths class, and a chain reaction took place, the climax of which came when Lexa was asked about integrals, as much a mystery to him as they were to me: both of them—teacher and student—maintained a three-minute silence, then Lexa received an 'F' and an official reprimand, noted in the record book, for disturbing the class.

During break, Lexa explained phallic symbol.

I stared at the golden waterfall undulating and sparkling a few paces ahead of us as we promenaded through the halls. 'But that's dumb,' I told him. 'It sure doesn't look like one.'

'But it's called a pony-tail, don't you see? "Tail" is a homonym for "cock".'

'Synonym,' said Berta, who as usual had done his homework.

'But it's just a word. It doesn't look a bit like the thing itself,' I said.

'Words can be erotic symbols too,' said Lexa. 'Like, Freud says that when you dream about a room, it really means a vagina.'

I thought about that for a moment, and then remembered a dream I'd had the night before, about how I was in church with Marie and—I quickly suppressed the rest of it and said, 'Bullshit. If that were true almost all our dreams would be—' I stopped, and then said, 'I'm always dreaming about being in some maths class with the teacher trying to prove I'm a mathematical idiot. Where's the vagina in that?'

'It's in the word,' said Lexa. 'In German, the word for woman is *Frauenzimmer*—in other words, a female chamber. And a chamber's a hollow space, like a vagina.'

'Then it's a linguistic problem, gentlemen,' said Harýk. 'Only Germans can be surrounded by cunts in their dreams. And maybe inhabitants of the *Ostmark*.'

'Why?' asked Benno. It was generally recognized that Benno was a little slow.

'What about "boudoir", maestro?' said Harýk, turning to him. 'Could that be a synonym for woman?'

'Depends on what a synonym is,' replied Benno.

'Or a homonym?' said Lexa.

'Boudoir and woman are not homonyms,' said Berta firmly.

My conscience was assuaged. Dreams of Marie in church were not immoral after all. Not in Czech, anyway.

And Marie was certainly in church right now. Her superb contralto voice was somewhere in all that wailing. I tried to pick it out but the church was too far away.

You are a jeeewel in God's heavenly crown . . .

sang the old women.

'Which one are you thinking about now, dreamer?' I heard Lexa say. Quickly I returned to the warehouse. Přema was standing in front of me, and he handed me a sheet of paper.

'Can you check my spelling, Danny?' he said. 'Make sure I didn't make mistakes.'

I took the document. *Brothers!* it began. *We haven't forgotten the events that happened a year ago at the Charles Univercity, when the student Jan Oplétal got shot—*

I corrected the mistakes and then said, 'You should add "Sisters".'

'What?' Přema said.

'Trust Smiřický to think of the *Frauenzimmers*,' said Lexa.

'You mean I should start it off "Brothers and Sisters"?' asked Přema. 'I don't think that's such a hot idea. Resistance isn't for girls.'

He took his fiery appeal, which amounted to an invitation to kill the Germans on sight, and went over to the corner where, in a box from the First Republic marked 'Czechoslovak Tobacco Board', he had hidden a small stencilling machine.

'So how come we told Kadeřábek to go ahead?' Nosek asked.

'That's different,' said Přema. 'Gerta has got serious reasons.'

Someone rapped out the pre-arranged signal on the warehouse door. Přema went to open it. Kadeřábek slipped into the room and sat down on the crate that Přema had just got up from. The murky light from a single bare lightbulb that hung on a wire from the ceiling made his features stand out. He looked like the mannequin in the window of the Paris Fashion House that Berta always dressed in a tux for the winter season, when there were a lot of formal dances in town. But Kadeřábek's masculine beauty was marred by a puffy lower lip, which he hadn't had when he'd gone off into the woods on his assignment. My lewd imagination placed its own interpretation on the puffy lip, and I found myself silently agreeing with Přema: women had no place in a resistance movement.

'Well?' said Přema.

Kadeřábek coughed.

'Will she or won't she?'

'I—uh—' said Kadeřábek, '—no.'

'What do you mean—no?' asked Harýk.

'She—uh—' said Kadeřábek, and again he coughed uneasily, as if to clear his throat.

W e had decided to drag Gerta Wotická into our resistance group because she'd had some trouble with Leopold Váňa, and Leopold Váňa didn't want anything to do with the resistance. Or perhaps he wanted to join but his father wouldn't let him, just as he wouldn't let him have anything to do with Gerta. That was what the trouble was all about.

Like everyone else, Váňa tried to make out with girls, but whereas my efforts along those lines came to nothing for reasons that were not clear to me (in the past year this had happened twenty-two times, each time with a different girl), the reasons why

Váňa had the same rate of success were as clear as day. He was, as one girl put it, boredom in trousers. (Precisely what she had in mind, or precisely what it was about him that bored her, she didn't say. Lexa professed to be morally outraged by her metaphor, if that's what it was.) But Irena told me that among the girls he'd tried to get anywhere with—and so far Váňa had tried it with only three, including Irena, so she spoke from personal experience— there was a general consensus that bordered on the telepathic. In addition, Váňa didn't look too good: he was as fat as Benno, but he didn't play an instrument, and he wore glasses with wire frames that hooked behind his ears.

But in the end he succeeded with Gerta, which wasn't really very surprising when you thought about it. Gerta was no Rachel, although both of them were avid swimmers. Gerta was good at high diving and Rachel was the district champion in the breast-stroke, both in and out of the water. But Rachel was a real beauty; she reminded me a little of Paulette Goddard in *Modern Times*. Gerta was a skinny girl and as far as breasts went, Benno—as Lexa put it—was two sizes bigger. She had pretty black eyes, but they were separated by a caricature of a nose—like the ones in the cartoons Rélink, the painter, started publishing just after the Germans established the Protectorate of Bohemia and Moravia. Rélink called himself an anti-Jew, an expression he'd obviously made up: right after we were annexed to the Reich, Czech was widely purged of foreign words, and I guess Rélink thought the expression 'anti-Semite' was too un-Czech. At the time, Lexa set up a club of pro-Jews, but it never got anywhere because Benno—who, as he said himself, was a half-Jew—refused to be president. Also, it soon became clear that anti-Jewishness wasn't a joke, the way the painter Rélink was a joke, so we quickly forgot about the club. Mainly, as a matter of fact, because of the trouble Gerta got into.

Anyway, Váňa finally made it with Gerta during the winter vacation in the Krkonoše Mountains in 1938, when Gerta saved his life. Váňa was a terrible skier. He couldn't go more than a few metres without falling and no one would ever go out on the slopes with him. One day while he was out alone, he fell and broke his leg, and of course he couldn't move. It happened in a ravine, right near a waterfall, so no one could hear his cries for help. A fog came

down and the rest of us retreated to the chalet. No one missed
Váňa until Gerta noticed he wasn't at supper because there were
dumplings left over. Meanwhile the fog had dispersed and the
slopes were sparkling in the starlight. We lit some torches and set
off to look for him. It was the first time we'd ever been on skis at
night, and with torches, at that. Lucie applied her torch to the seat
of Harýk's pants, making him yelp, then we all started fooling
around with the torches and forgot about Váňa again. Marie was
pointing up in the sky at Venus with exaggerated interest, with a
finger gloved in pink wool, and I was just looking up at the planet of
love when I caught sight of a flickering flame quickly descending
into the ravine by the waterfall. Gerta. Perhaps they were destined
for each other.

But they weren't. Though it seemed that way at first, both
socially and sexually. Mr Váňa and Mr Wotický owned the two
biggest textile stores in Kostelec; one of them had an only son, the
other an only daughter; the daughter was no Aphrodite and the son
was no Adonis, more like Hephaestus (particularly after his skiing
accident, which gave him a limp). It looked like a serious
relationship—a little premature, perhaps, since Váňa was only in
the sixth form and Gerta in the fifth, but that was hardly
exceptional. That summer one of Gerta's classmates, Libuše,
Šafránková, who also was no Aphrodite, got married a day after
she turned sixteen. Not that she had to, but her father, Dr
Guth-Moravský, was pushing eighty and was afraid he wouldn't
last till the plums ripened. It was an open secret in Kostelec that
Mr Šafránek, the head-waiter of the Beránek Café, wasn't
Libuše's father, although he purported to be, just as he wasn't the
father of her older sister Teta, who'd got married the year before, a
day after she graduated from high school—nor of her eldest sister,
Kazi, who had to wait a full year after graduation before Dr
Guth-Moravský finally managed to get her hitched. In her case, of
course, he wasn't in any hurry; at the time he was only seventy-
five and still took part in the Christmas polar-bear marathon swim
in the Vltava River. And it was obvious to everyone in Kostelec
that the head-waiter hadn't built his villa below Černá Hora,
designed by a famous Prague architect, from the money he made
on tips. Even if there were people gullible enough to believe it, they

219

might well have wondered why all three of the girls with pagan names were as ugly as night, when their father was an elegantly handsome man with a Clark Gable moustache and their mother, now in her early forties, looked like an eighteen-year-old model from Rosenbaum's fashion salon in Prague. The gullible, had they wondered, might have explained it as a freak of nature, but the rest of us knew why: the President's Master of Ceremonies, Dr Guth-Moravský, looked like those paintings of troglodytes in anthropology textbooks. As well as being the author of a famous manual of social etiquette, Dr Guth-Moravský had written a work called *The Mores and Customs of Czech Paganism*, which explained why he'd named his daughters after women from old Czech legends. It was also whispered that he had accumulated his fortune not as a famous man of letters or from his salary as Master of Ceremonies, but as a marriage-broker for the old Austro-Bohemian aristocrats.

So a serious relationship between a girl from the fifth form and a boy from the sixth was more a rule than an exception at the Kostelec high school. We had some shining examples in the band. Benno had been going with Alena since the third form, but it was Harýk who had broken all the records of this odd tradition. In the spring of '38, after the municipal physician, Dr Eichler, conducted his annual check-up of the students, he summoned the architect, Mr Hartmann—who was Lucie's father—to his office. When Hartmann came home, Lucie's brother told us, he took a belt to her without a word of explanation and then put her under house arrest for three months, which was, of course, too late to save her virginity. The reason didn't remain a mystery for long because Dr Eichler's son, who was studying Latin and was bored to tears, had heard Mr Hartmann through his father's office door lamenting his daughter's fate, and of course he couldn't keep such sensational news to himself. At the time, Lucie was in the second form and Harýk in the fourth.

Gerta and Váňa had a serious relationship, but whether it was true love or not was another matter. It looked more to me like making a virtue of necessity. Although I wasn't really capable of understanding something like that—since of course all twenty-two of my attempts had been made when I was in love, at least while the attempt lasted—I knew such things existed, because people aren't all the same, except insofar as they're all after that one thing. So I supposed it wasn't passion that kept them together, but simply the fact that Váňa couldn't get anyone else, that and Gerta—

That was another one of the open secrets of the Kostelec high school: of all the girls who had fallen for the magic of Kadeřábek's mannequin beauty, Gerta had fallen the hardest. And if all the victims were suffering from colour-blindness, Gerta was living in a permanent fog—or rather, in the heart of a Babylonian darkness. From the third form on, Kadeřábek had been fast friends with František Buřtoch, despite the fact that Buřtoch was ten years older. Buřtoch's father, a butcher, had disinherited his son when, upon completing his butcher's apprenticeship, František had set up a business in antiques and *objets d'art* using money left him by a bachelor friend. So the thing was obvious, but not to those colour-blind girls, who secretly, with hard-won money, bribed a photographer to sell them studio portraits of Kadeřábek. In short, love had blinded them, or perhaps they'd been raised so correctly that the truth about Kadeřábek's preferences had simply eluded them, though I knew them too well to really believe that.

Kadeřábek was indeed a perverse Adonis. Instead of playing tennis, he was a shot-put ace for the Kostelec Sports Club, which was also why athletics suddenly became so popular with the girls that Kostelec had the largest club of young female hopefuls in the entire district, and also the best, because otherwise there wasn't much competition in women's athletics. The only girl who drove herself around the cinder track because she really liked doing it was Irena, but she was perverse about it too. Otherwise the girls would jog around the soccer field or leap into the long-jump pits for reasons that were clear, if not low and immoral. Marie, unfortunately, was not one of them, although I'd have loved to see her in shorts. Perhaps her boyfriend had emotionally neutralized her.

Gerta had done high diving since she'd been a little girl and now, having succumbed to the magic of Kadeřábek, she took up the high jump and eventually broke the junior women's record. But it didn't do her any good. The day when she made a name for herself came later: the heavy shot slipped out of Kadeřábek's hand and fell behind him, and Gerta rushed out of the crowd of admiring girls, picked the shot up, and ran to return it to the astonished athlete.

It was as clear as day.

But whether this was passion or not, in the autumn of '39 Gerta didn't come to school for two days, and when she finally showed up her beauty carried another blemish: her large nose now glowed like a peony and there were big red circles around her pretty black eyes. Váňa stopped waiting for her after school, and on Saturday he came into the Beránek alone for the tea dance and tried to dance with Alena, but he stepped so hard on her shoes that she cried out, and he then sat by himself until the end of the dance, glowering into his lemonade.

Because we weren't very fond of him, and because Gerta looked so miserable, we went over to his table during the *Jauzepause* and Lexa spoke to him:

'What did you do to her, you murderer?'

'Nothing. I stepped on her corns. It could happen to anyone.'

'I'm not talking about Alena. Don't tell me you don't know who I mean!'

Vana said nothing.

'Well, sir, are you going to explain yourself?' said Harýk.

'It's not my fault,' said Váňa.

'She gave you the gate, right?'

'No, she didn't.'

'Then how come you ditched her? You were just stringing her along, weren't you?'

'No, I wasn't,' said Váňa.

We looked at each other and shook our heads.

'OK, then. If she didn't come across, that's your fault. You had a year and a half to work on it. But that's still no reason for you to shit on her.'

'I didn't shit on her.'

'So how come you're not going out with her any more? Can't you see the poor girl's suffering?' said Lexa.

Váňa was silent again.

'What lies are you concocting now, sir?' asked Harýk.

Suddenly Váňa blurted out: 'She's a Jew!'

We were floored. That was when we realized that all this anti-Semitic stuff wasn't a joke any more. But how could Váňa be such a jerk?

'You hardly seem a zealous enough Catholic, sir, to object to the religious affiliation of your bedmate,' said Harýk.

'It's got nothing to do with religion,' wailed Váňa. 'You know what this is all about.'

'Do we know what this is all about, gentlemen?' asked Harýk, looking around at us. We all shook our heads.

'It doesn't bother me a bit, seriously,' said Váňa quickly. 'But my old man—'

There are some fools in the world who obey the fourth commandment to the letter so their days may be long on this earth. Their thoughts should be on heaven, but they're not. We couldn't get Váňa to budge. Probably he had nothing personal against Gerta. But he wanted his days to be long on this earth, just like his old man.

So Kadeřábek was queer, but otherwise he was ready for any mischief. The students of Moses' faith still went to the high school, but from the way things were going it was pretty clear that even the Jews in the eighth form wouldn't make it to matriculation. Soon after Váňa ditched her, Gerta had to sew a yellow star over her negligible breasts, but that was after her second, and worse, disaster. Then Mrs Mánesová began wearing a star, and Rachel too, except that by the end of 1938, at least according to Father Meloun's records, she was married to Tonda Kratochvíl. For the longest time only Father Meloun knew about it, because it had been a secret wedding. Why it was secret when the parish records said it had taken place in '38, back during the First Republic, wasn't clear. The explanation came in '41 when we were rehearsing at the school revue, but that's another story. Benno kept attending school even after the stars started appearing, and so did his sister Věra, because they were only half-Jews. I began to like Věra more and more, but I didn't try my luck with her a second time (although otherwise I had nothing against second and third and sometimes even fourth and fifth attempts, and, in the case of Marie and Irena, I'd lost track because there were no computers in those days). But not for the same reason that Váňa had dumped Gerta. Even people of mixed race were beginning to feel the heat now, because at any moment the Germans could up the 'racial awareness' ante, though God knew when. And I didn't want Věra to think I was exploiting the situation or taking an interest in her as an act of mercy, or that I was trying to silence a bad Aryan conscience, since I was, well, an Aryan. I didn't know. I wasn't sure why I was so reluctant. I was just a jerk. But a different kind from Váňa.

I also can't remember who first got the idea. Whoever it was, he got it after Kadeřábek, of all people, came up with the notion of starting a resistance movement. It's hard to say which idea was more stupid. When I told Přema about it, he swore me to silence and then told me that they already had a resistance movement, of people in trades, and that he, Přema, was the leader. Přema had originally been a student at the business academy, but after 1939, out of pure patriotism, he'd refused to learn German. In fact, the teacher couldn't get a single word of German out of him, so the principal quickly expelled him from the academy. In his own interest, he went to explain it personally to Přema's father, Mr Skočdopole. At first Mr Skočdopole, as a former legionnaire, was somewhat crusty with him. But then, as an alcoholic, he pulled out a bottle of home-made slivovice, a gift from his brother in Moravia, and they both got drunk under a portrait of President Masaryk, from which Mr Skočdopole had removed, for the occasion, a picture of Božena Němcová with which he'd covered up Masaryk with when the Protectorate was declared. Finally they both agreed that Přema had it coming to him, and then they fell asleep. Now Přema decided that we should combine the groups so we'd have connections with the intellectuals as well as ordinary people, and one idea led to another until finally someone said we should also have connections with the Jews, who happened to have the best reasons for getting mixed up in a resistance movement, and as a final idea, someone said, 'Gerta.'

'We can rely on her,' said Nosek. 'In a way, she's already been hit by the German laws.'

DON'T ▸ AVOID ▸ THE ▸ ISSUES

Subscribe to Granta and you need never miss another issue. You'll get free delivery to your home and save up to 28% off the bookshop price!

Name

Address

Postcode

BI291

Please enter my subscription for:
☐ one year £16　☐ two years £30　☐ three years £43

Please start my subscription with issue number _____

Payment:
☐ cheque enclosed　☐ I will pay later: please bill me
☐ Access/American Express/Diners Club no:

(Please note: we cannot accept Visa/Barclaycard)

OVERSEAS POSTAGE. Europe: please add £4 per year. Outside Europe: £8 per year air-speeded, £12 per year airmail.

UP TO 28% OFF

DON'T ▸ AVOID ▸ THE ▸ ISSUES

Subscribe to Granta and you need never miss another issue. You'll get free delivery to your home and save up to 28% off the bookshop price!

Name

Address

Postcode

BI292

Please enter my subscription for:
☐ one year £16　☐ two years £30　☐ three years £43

Please start my subscription with issue number _____

Payment:
☐ cheque enclosed　☐ I will pay later: please bill me
☐ Access/American Express/Diners Club no:

(Please note: we cannot accept Visa/Barclaycard)

OVERSEAS POSTAGE. Europe: please add £4 per year. Outside Europe: £8 per year air-speeded, £12 per year airmail.

UP TO 28% OFF

No postage necessary if posted in the UK

Granta
FREEPOST
Cambridge
CB1 1BR

No postage necessary if posted in the UK

Granta
FREEPOST
Cambridge
CB1 1BR

'But she's a girl,' objected Přema.

'Well—' said Lexa, and he was going to continue, but then stopped and said, '—as a matter of fact, she is.'

'Girls are timid,' said Přema.

'Sure they are!' said Harýk. 'Look, would you have the guts to dive off a thirty-foot tower?'

'I can't swim,' said Přema.

'Lord!' said Harýk.

We were silent. Then Kadeřábek said, 'In a democratic state girls are equal. And according to physiological research, they can stand more punishment than men, relatively speaking.'

This sounded strange coming from him. The short sleeves on his elegant shirt were not enough to cover his bulging biceps.

'But not emotionally,' said Lexa.

'Bullshit. Look at Joan of Arc,' said Nosek.

We were silent again. Then I said, 'A girl who's not afraid to dive from a thirty-foot tower must have a pretty good set of nerves.'

In the end we decided that Gerta, girl or not, must have nerves like Tarzan, and that furthermore, because of that jerk Váňa, she'd been the first in the school to suffer the consequences of Nazism, so she had better reasons for doing this than we did.

The next question was who would talk to her.

'Wee Daniel, of course,' said Harýk. 'He's the champion talker.'

'But he's not the champion persuader,' said Lexa. 'At least not of ladies.'

By this time my embarrassing reputation had ceased to bother me.

Then came the final idea, the most brilliant of all, and I was the one who had it. 'I have someone better in mind.'

'Who? Berta?' asked Lexa. Berta involuntarily twitched and blushed.

'No,' I said. 'Květomil.'

Květomil was Kadeřábek's first name. An appropriate name at that. Flower-lover.

'Gentlemen—' Kadeřábek was clearly taken aback. 'I'm not—I mean, that kind of thing's not my—my cup of tea.'

225

'This is politics, not erotics, sir,' said Lexa.

'Besides that, you're the chairman,' I said. 'Or I mean the commander.'

'And Gerta's always had a crush on you,' said Harýk. 'Remember the time she brought you back the shot-put?'

'Go ahead and have your fun,' said Kadeřábek. 'I don't mind. But it's not my cup of tea.'

'I repeat: it's a matter of politics, not erotics,' said Harýk.

'Or of politics through erotics,' I said, 'and the end justifies the means.'

Because we were a democratic resistance movement, we put the matter to a vote, and decided that Květomil would be the one to establish contact with Gerta.

He tried next day during the lunch-break. That morning an embarrassing situation arose during the first lesson, which was German. Ilse Seligerová stood up and asked Miss Althammerová to make Gerta sit in the back row. Ilse had been sitting beside Gerta since the first form. She was German and preferred speaking German to Czech. Miss Althammerová was a German too, but even so she asked Ilse, '*Warum den?*'

'*Sie wissen doch, Fräulein Doktor,*' replied Ilse icily.

Miss Althammerová turned red, took a deep breath, then let it out again and said, in a quiet voice, '*Na gut—wenn Gerta nichts dagegen hat.*'

Gerta burst into tears and ran to the back row where the overweight Petridesová sat. The classroom was as silent as a tomb. I saw Petridesová give Gerta her handkerchief.

Petridesová was walking through the halls beside Gerta during the lunch-break when Květomil joined them, perspiring. Petridesová played the fifth wheel for a while, then discreetly went off to the girls' washroom. With a shiny face, Květomil promenaded around the halls with Gerta, speaking to her while she raised her red-rimmed eyes to him. When the bell rang, I saw that the shot-put champion was smiling.

'So, what happened?' asked Harýk.

'Well—I established contact,' said Květomil.

'And—is she for it?'

'We didn't get that far. I have to sound her out first, don't I?'
'Oh, Lord. And how did you "sound her out"?'
'Well, we talked about movies and—'
'And what?'
'And so on,' said Květomil.
'And then?'
'And then the bell rang.'
So the first contact was just reconnoitring.

In the week that followed, Květomil must have discussed the entire history of the cinema with Gerta, because he couldn't think of anything else to talk about. Gerta's gaze became more and more amorous. He could have talked to her about bowel disease, or even about the resistance, and Gerta wouldn't have minded. The red circles around her beautiful eyes vanished, and her nose regained its accustomed whiteness. But they never got beyond what Květomil called 'sounding out'. Finally, at the end of the week, he said, 'I can't do it in school. I'll have to invite her somewhere.'

'You should have done that long ago, you jerk,' said Lexa.
'Take her to the movies,' said Harýk.
'That's even worse than school.'
'Make a date to see her in the woods,' I said. 'No one will hear what you say there.'

And so Květomil invited Gerta to meet him in the woods in a small meadow called By the Cottage—although the cottage, which had once belonged to a shepherd, was in ruins. The meadow was overgrown with an aromatic moss—not long before, I had tried to intoxicate Irena with its perfume. In vain, of course.

From the window of Mánes's villa we watched as Květomil— in corduroy trousers and one of his elegant shirts, beneath which his cultivated muscles rippled—strode into the forest. After ten minutes Gerta walked across the bridge to the brewery. She was wearing a Sunday dress.

L ater we sat in the warehouse and waited for Květomil, and possibly for Gerta, if he'd managed to persuade her. Time dragged and this didn't augur well. Or perhaps it did. Finally Květomil himself showed up and said, 'I—uh—no.'

'Wait a minute,' said Harýk. 'What do you mean, no?'

227

'She—' said Květomil—and delicately, he touched his tellingly swollen lip, which I had misinterpreted.

So I don't know. I guess we made a mistake. We chose the wrong tactics. We were young and stupid. We held the glories of this world in contempt, but we had no antennae. Three years later—where did Gerta end up? Back then, she could probably think things through more clearly than I could, than Lexa could. Everything. The resistance and love. Anyway, our resistance group faded away too, and for all I know it may have had something to do with Gerta. Only Přema stuck to it, probably because at the time he hadn't understood anything at all. Přema wasn't much for the girls, though for different reasons to Květomil. He was naturally shy, he didn't understand girls and was even afraid of them. I wasn't afraid of them, but did I understand them? It had been my dumb idea to use her queer idol to persuade her to join us. So I didn't understand girls worth a damn either.

We could still hear the old women singing in the church.

The jewel of all the heaaavens thou aaaaart. . .

I no longer tried to make out Marie's sweet voice in that infernal, or perhaps heavenly, wailing.

'She what?' asked Harýk.

'Well,' said Květomil, 'I didn't want to come right out with it, so I began to—' He stopped.

'Don't tell me,' said Lexa. 'You talked about movies.'

'No, about athletics. Then about swimming,' said Květomil.

'Wonderful,' said Harýk, looking at his watch. 'God, how can swimming and the shot-put take up four hours of anyone's time! That must be a district record. Maybe even a world record!'

'We talked about literature too,' said Květomil.

'Now that could only have taken you five minutes,' I said. I knew that the only printed matter Květomil ever read was the illustrated sports weekly *Start*.

'And then about politics,' said Květomil.

'And did you tell her what you were supposed to?' asked Harýk impatiently.

'I began slowly so I wouldn't frighten her, right?' said Květomil. 'I said I'd been watching her for a long time, and that of all the girls at school she'd always seemed to me kind of—'

'Kind of what?' said Harýk.

'Kind of—the most mature. And—and the most interesting.'

I could imagine them there in the tiny meadow, sitting on that aromatic moss that almost, but not quite, intoxicated Irena. I could see Gerta hanging on Květomil the Adonis with her beautiful Jewish eyes—and suddenly I realized what the mistake had been. Of course. Gerta hadn't paid much attention to his talk about the shot-put. She was in fifth heaven when they sat down on the moss, in sixth when she breathed in its aroma, and when he started babbling on about how she was the most mature and the most interesting of all the girls in the school, she arrived in seventh heaven. Then she was overwhelmed by that feeling they write about in novels, and she flew to him, as they say, on the wings of love, and cleaved to him in a long, passionate kiss until his lip swelled up, and he never managed to blurt out his more important message to her.

Thou art the jewel of hiiiiighest heaven . . .

'Well, and then I said it,' I heard Květomil say. 'That we'd decided to invite her into our resistance group—'

And again, for the tenth time, he fell silent.

'And what did she say?' Harýk blurted out.

For a moment, Květomil looked as though he'd just tumbled out of the sky.

'She slapped my face,' he said. 'And then she ran away.'

A silence fell over the warehouse. The only sound was the singing of the old women in the church on the square.

'You can't figure women out,' said Květomil. 'At least I sure can't.'

Translated from the Czech by Paul Wilson

229

Thought for food.

ROBERT FISK

BEIRUT DIARY

Wednesday 26 April 1989

The nun beside me on the helicopter this morning had a tight, self-righteous face. People who have found a cause in Lebanon produce this face. The Shia Muslim imams in southern Lebanon stare at you and seem to be saying: I am right, I am a good person fighting for justice and decency.

I told the nun I was a journalist working for the London *Independent*, and I asked what she was doing.

'Taking medicine to children in the hospitals,' she shouted above the din of the engine. As if anxious to convince me, she opened the lid of a small box beside her feet to reveal bottles of ointment and pills.

I asked her name.

Her face frosted over. 'I never give my name when I am on a dangerous mission.' I knew that her mission was not really dangerous. Not yet.

The Lebanese Army Puma thumped through the hot morning air. The coastline appeared through the haze to our left. According to the news agencies—who have developed an art of smothering interest in Lebanon by reporting it from Cyprus—it had been a week in which 'Syrian and Christian gunners pounded both sides of Beirut with howitzers and Soviet-made Grad multi-barrelled rocket-launchers.' Note 'Soviet-made'. The Evil Empire may be crumbling but it thrives in the wire agencies.

Our helicopter belonged to General Michel Aoun's faction of the Lebanese Army and made a perfect target for those Soviet-made Grad multi-barrelled rocket-launchers. In a feature film, the coastline and mountains of Lebanon would be covered in smoke from exploding shells. But this was not a film, and the Lebanese coast basked in the spring sunshine, displaying bright greens and yellow ochres. The red-roofed Levantine houses along the sea front seemed as neat and prosperous as they had to T. E. Lawrence when he praised their symmetry and tastefulness.

At the landing-site an army lieutenant stood by a small school desk. A group of unshaven taxi-men waited behind barbed wire. 'Have you come to see our war?' the lieutenant asked me. 'We have had 1,000 shells here.' The soldiers around him, in camouflage fatigues and ungroomed moustaches, giggled. The nun put her passport on the table. When she saw me reading her name, she grabbed it back and turned to me with a scowl.

The taxi-man charged twenty-six dollars for the drive to the Aquarium Hotel. The hotel languishes on the sea front, its front door sandbagged, its holiday guests a memory, its gloomy blue-uniformed staff standing in a deserted front lobby. There had been no electricity for two days.

'Mr Robert!' Tannious called. He remembered me from six months before. He smiled his gap-toothed smile, grabbed my suitcase and limped off.

Maurice Sayegh, the Aquarium's manager, remembered me too. 'Please, Robert, don't pay in American Express this time. They take two months to pay us back.' He was happy this morning. There had been no shelling overnight. 'Two nights ago,' Maurice explained, 'three Grads came down outside the hotel. One blew up a car. Another hit our gardener. He was picking tomatoes. It actually hit him. The missile cut him in half. Clean in half. There was a French TV crew with us. They filmed everything.'

Thursday 27 April

The Arab League in Tunis announced a cease-fire in Lebanon. I thought, why not see General Aoun today?

The voice on the telephone from the Lebanese presidential palace was polite but adamant and with a hint of the nun's self-righteousness. No, the general was very busy. 'I promise you he will see you tomorrow at eleven a.m.'

I started to whine; this had worked before. My editor wanted me to see the general today, to get his reaction to the announcement from Tunis. A Friday interview would be too late. I had come to Lebanon only to see the general.

The official didn't care. 'Eleven a.m. tomorrow.'

Friday 28 April

General Aoun was smaller than I had expected. He could not be seen above the heads of his staff.

His shell-proof bunker used to be part of the underground car-park of the presidential palace. Outside there was a pile of shell fragments collected from the palace forecourt, mementoes of the night's shelling by the Syrians.

Aoun was dressed in American combat fatigues. His face was drawn. Dark rims ringed his eyes, which were bloodshot. He blinked frequently. He had been directing artillery batteries all night. For six weeks he had been living in the bunker and he had the appearance of a mole emerging from a long sleep. Apparatchiks in blue suits and ties fluttered about, whispering 'Monsieur Le President' in Aoun's ear when they wanted to catch his attention. His daughter sat beside his desk and fumbled with a tape-recorder, an adoring look on her face. The Napoleon of Lebanon was about to speak from his underground garage; my eleven a.m. appointment had turned out to be a press conference.

Aoun wanted a westernized Lebanon. 'Like France, like America.' He could not see why this might not suit the Muslims. He claimed to represent them. What if his 'war of liberation' against Syria failed? someone asked. He responded with a lecture on the inevitable triumph of all wars of liberation. 'History shows this,' he said, sitting back with a look of satisfaction. 'Look at the French Maquis in the Second World War, the Algerian resistance to the French, the Vietcong.' I asked him what his plans were.

There was a long pause. 'Plans? What plans?'

Monday 1 May

I was sitting on the balcony trying to read by candle-light when I saw flames rise from the sea. An explosion followed. In video-taped news reports of shelling or bombing in Lebanon, the technicians synchronize the sound of a detonation with the visual image of the explosion. In real life you see the fall of shot and hear it afterwards. I have always suspected that a lot of people get killed in wars because they have spent too much time watching war movies on television. They see an explosion but don't believe it's really happening because they have yet to hear the sound. They don't take cover.

In 1982 I watched Israeli jets bomb houses in Beirut. The

235

planes dived, a small black rugby ball dropped from the wing and an entire apartment block disappeared in grey smoke and crumpled to the ground. Not a sound.

In Jounieh, the missiles were landing only a hundred metres away. The bang came less than a second after the flash. The change in air pressure sent me crawling across the floor into the bathroom. I heard a hiss but it was only my ears, which felt as if they had been boxed repeatedly. Up on the mountainside above the Aquarium a great fire was progressing through the fir trees. In the field where the gardener was cut in half, hundreds of frogs croaked in choral unison.

Wednesday 3 May

This afternoon, the two Arab League envoys to Lebanon, Assistant Secretary-General Lakhdar Ibrahimi and the Kuwaiti ambassador to Syria, announced that the League's truce was in effect. More than a hundred 'observers' were to come to Beirut to guarantee the cease-fire.

I met Ibrahimi after his announcement. He was friendly and seemed well-intentioned. He spoke English beautifully. 'There is now no reason for anyone to fire a single shell again in Lebanon,' he said into my microphone. I wanted to believe this statement, although I knew it was preposterous. I didn't challenge him and instead asked which Arab states would contribute to the League's observer force. Jordan and Kuwait; a good army and a poor one.

Thursday 4 May

The morning papers carried Ibrahimi's promises across their front pages. They also mentioned that there had been casualties from the rockets that had fallen above Jounieh. A woman had been killed in her home. Members of her family had been badly hurt. But the cease-fire was holding.

I drove to east Beirut and visited the Foreign Ministry. In Beirut the best way of meeting a dignitary is to turn up unannounced and explain that broken telephone lines prevented making an appointment. This white lie works because it reflects the truth. Within five minutes, I was sitting with Farouk Abillama, the director-general of the Foreign Ministry. He was a Christian Maronite, an aristocrat. He had little hope that the Arab League's cease-fire guarantors would ever come to Beirut. He would have liked an international peace-keeping force to be stationed from the southernmost to the northernmost frontiers of the country. And I thought the Arab League proposal was unrealistic.

Lunch with an old acquaintance at the Au Vieux Quartier restaurant in the heart of east Beirut. There were sandbags against the back windows. Otherwise it could have been Paris. Smoked salmon, artichoke hearts, roast lamb, a bottle of Ksara '68, Lebanon's finest red wine, waiters in black jackets. Most of the diners were probably bankers. Banks still thrive in Beirut because the militias are paid in dollars. Lebanese currency is so inflated that bills are figured in dollars. Lebanese businessmen pay for imports in dollars, ask for dollars from their customers. The economic collapse, the 'dollarization' of commerce, began when Western troops withdrew in 1984.

After lunch I drove past what used to be the Beirut classical museum. It stands about 400 yards into the Christian side of the front line. Quotation from Hachette's *Guide to Lebanon*, 1965: 'The showcases are arranged in chronological order, so as to make clearer to the visitor the evolution of civilization in Lebanon.' The museum's façade has been smashed by shrapnel and scored by thousands of bullets. Its treasures were long ago withdrawn and relocated, but in the trees to my left, amid piles of garbage and sandbags, I could see the wreckage of great Phoenician sarcophagi.

A friend was waiting for me at the museum. A Lebanese Christian Maronite soldier waved us through and our car raced up the empty road towards west Beirut and the Syrian line. We heard the hissing of cicadas when we drew up at the other end of the street. Syrian troops stood alongside Lebanese Muslim troops. The Syrians were dressed in US Marine camouflage fatigues, like Aoun's soldiers. But their helmets were Soviet and not of the latest design. Maybe left over from Stalingrad.

Aoun and his supporters portray the Syrians as the source of all evil in Lebanon. They tell you that the Syrians will arrange for the kidnap of any Westerner in Beirut. If the Syrians left Lebanon, the country would return to democracy. The reality is not so simple. When I travel in west Beirut, I drive with the doors locked, the windows closed, for fear of kidnappers. So when I see Syrian troops, I feel safer. Before the Syrians returned to west Beirut in February 1987 (they had arrived in 1976 and were ejected by the Israeli army in 1982), I lived in fear. Every Westerner was a target for kidnappers. Lebanese militia units fought each other. The Syrians returned and forced the gunmen from the streets. When I see the Syrians today, I *do* feel safer. Who wants to be kidnapped in the interests of democracy?

Friday 5 May

At four this afternoon I went to see Selim el-Hoss, Lebanon's Muslim prime minister and Aoun's rival. Like Aoun, he had a pile of scrap metal outside his office, the results of the night's shelling by the Lebanese army. It was as if the two men were competing in their contempt for the other's weaponry. There was a notice on the door politely requesting visitors to leave their guns outside. Hoss arrived, apologizing for being ten minutes late. He was a tall, professional man. Like Aoun a week ago, he sat next to a Lebanese flag. A photograph of his daughter was displayed on a table.

'What we need is a meeting of Parliament that will create a new president and put Aoun and myself out of existence.' Hoss did not talk about wars of liberation. 'We must have a meeting of Parliament to elect a president and at the very same sitting there will be a debate for a speaker and a debate on political reform. This is what lies at the heart of our problem.'

What about the Syrian army, which Aoun had sworn to evict from Lebanon?

'Why talk about this now? We need political reform. After this, we can talk about sovereignty.' Aoun had said he wanted the Syrians out before political concessions were made; Hoss wanted political concessions before the Syrians left. Hoss appeared uncomfortable when I asked if he was not merely a pawn of the Syrians. 'Have you seen any Syrians outside my office? They do not tell me what to say. They do not pay me daily visits to dictate my words. They come sometimes to me as representatives of

Syria. But I am free.'
   In Lebanon no one is free. The structure of power—social,
political, military—rests upon mutual threat rather than mutual
trust. Lebanon functioned on family consensus—on an unspoken
agreement between the great families (Chamoun, Jumblatt,
Gemayel, Franjieh, Salaam). Now it exists on a basis of military
balance. Militias fight to a standstill, never to victory. Neither the
Syrians nor Aoun have taken a square inch of territory from each
other.

Saturday 6 May

I spent all day and all night in the Associated Press bureau in west
Beirut. The office includes Lebanese of almost every religious
denomination: Farouk is a Sunni, Charles a Maronite, Janine in
the photo section is a Shiite, Hussein the driver is a Kurd. There
are two Protestants, one Greek Catholic, one Armenian, three
Shiites and four Sunnis. In theory, they should be at war with each
other. In practice, they constitute the only office I have ever
visited in Beirut where the staff protect each other. If only the
Hosses and the Aouns could spend a few days in the satisfying
chaos of the AP, they might learn something about the real
Lebanon of which they both aspire to be leaders.
   Shells began falling around the building a few minutes after I
walked in. 'Don't worry, Fiskovitch, you may use our telex. You
are welcome here. We will look after you.' Farouk, who often
adopts an air of funereal seriousness at moments of great danger,
announced that it would be 'a bad night'. Then the surface broke:
'Charles has some *kibbiniyeh* for our meal tonight. We have
fifteen-year-old Scotch whisky. You will stay with us.' The whole
building was shaking to the blast of explosions. I would spend the
night sleeping on a mattress which Charles had prepared in the
office which used to belong to Terry Anderson, the American AP
bureau chief who was kidnapped four years ago.
   I woke up when a rocket crashed into a neighbouring building.
I turned on the light and I saw that the wall was covered with
photographs of Terry. On the left was the Terry I remembered,
enthusiastic, grinning, his spectacles making his eyes seem smaller

than they are. To the right was the other Terry, the one I did not know, staring from his basement at his kidnappers' cameras and videotape machines. Terry frightened, his eyes wide with anxiety, Terry angry, talking into a video, asking why President Reagan could not negotiate his release. Terry tired, weak, a weed-like moustache weighing down his cheeks. Did I know the other Terry? He could not be far away. He could probably hear the shells that were exploding around me.

Sunday 7 May

Lunch with friends, Shiites from southern Lebanon, in their stiflingly hot apartment on Hamra Street. They bought pizza and served warm beer and Pepsi. A thin-faced young man rose from the sofa to go to the dining-table, and a small black pistol fell from his belt. He quickly threw a cushion over the gun. We talked about prospects for a political settlement, about Lebanon's propensity for self-destruction.

Monday 8 May

So many shells fell around the AP bureau that I could only make one quick trip to the supermarket on Sadat Street. Hussein drove like a Grand Prix competitor, choosing routes through the narrowest streets with the highest buildings to avoid falling shells. We came out of the market holding plastic bags of bread, cheese and wine.

A round hit a building thirty feet from the AP, causing Farouk to abandon his computer screen and seek sanctuary with us in a little alcove where newspaper files are kept. I realized how far out on the edge of a razor these reporters work. If the gunner had leaned for a couple of seconds against his weapon—or if the wind had changed direction high above Beirut in the path of the shell— the round might have come through our window.

Saturday 13 May

I found victims of the Arab League's cease-fire at the Pasteur Hospital in Jounieh this morning. The Sfeir family had been in their underground shelter watching the television news on Thursday night and heard Lakhdar Ibrahimi announce that there was no reason for anyone to fire another shell in Lebanon. They emerged from their shelter and headed up the road to their bungalow for dinner. The meal was already in the cooker when a Grad missile (fired by the Syrians from west Beirut) came clean through the window, decapitating Nadia Sfeir and blasting her family around the room. Nadia died with her fifteen-month-old son Chadi in her arms.

In hospital, Chadi lay in pain, shrieking and crying and whimpering, his half-severed fingers bleeding into a great swathe of bandages. His older brother Charbel had scars over his arms, and his uncle, Joseph, a collection of huge black scabs over his face and chest. 'If Aoun wins, this will have been worth it,' he said.

I drove up to the Sfeir family's wrecked villa on the hillside. There were remains of a child's piano, of Charbel's latest school report. The neighbours produced a book of snapshots which they had salvaged from the rubble. Nadia at Chadi's christening, a big, slightly overweight woman with a gentle face. Charbel holding Chadi on his lap with an embarrassed smile. I had heard the missile explode two evenings before, while sitting with some Italian journalists in a bar. 'So much for the cease-fire,' one of the Italians had said.

When I returned to my hotel from the ruined house, the same Italian was standing at the reception desk. 'They've just kidnapped an Englishman in west Beirut,' he said. 'Guy called Jackie Mann, used to be an airline pilot. He's 75.' Jackie Mann used to be an RAF fighter pilot. He could not convince himself to leave Lebanon. He found work as a barman in west Beirut. He and his elderly wife had waited for things to get better, like the Lebanese.

Thursday 18 May

A relief to be away from the city. I was at Ayoun Es-Simaan, at the very top of the Mount Lebanon range. There was snow up there, and the air was so thin that my lungs began to hurt. The Phalangists were bundled in furs. The Syrians occupied a ridge of hills opposite, their dug-outs clearly visible in the silver light. The mountains securely enclosed us, brown and white peaks jutting above the blue mist. Here, perhaps, was a Lebanon that was worth fighting for, a serene, beautiful place.

Monday 22 May

Flew to southern Lebanon this morning in a United Nations helicopter to spend two days with the Finnish UN battalion. More territory that was worth fighting for. The hills were covered with heather and wild flowers, pink and gold bushes. Many butterflies. Soldiers from Helsinki and Turku drove around in armoured vehicles that had been made for fighting in the permafrost of the Arctic. The Finns had a sauna in every company position. The commanding officer's sauna was a great log cabin equipped with a fridge full of beer.

You could smell the flowers and the long grass. A large buzzard circled us as we crossed from 'liberated Lebanon' (controlled by Lebanese guerrillas) into 'free Lebanon' (the area occupied by the Israelis and their allies). We stopped at a small house where a Lebanese Shia couple described how one of their sons had been blackmailed into joining the pro-Israeli militia. He had been threatened with deportation if he refused. Now that he had joined the militia, the whole family was under threat of assassination from the Hezbollah.

Wednesday 24 May

Back to Beirut in the UN helicopter. The Mediterranean was thick with untreated sewage and garbage. The filth is washing up on to neighbouring shores. In Cyprus, Syria, Israel, Turkey, they are complaining about the muck from Lebanon. When I looked down from the helicopter—so far out that I could no longer see the coast—the country's detritus lay thick across the water. Boxes, paper, metal canisters, wood and brown slime, mile after mile of it spreading into the sea, staining the waves.

Wednesday 21 June

Damascus. The swimming-pool coffee-bar at the Sheraton Hotel.

Only twelve miles from the Lebanese border, only sixty miles from the Beirut war—it could have been a thousand miles away. French wine, astronomical prices, air-conditioning.

Lieutenant-General Mustapha Tlass, Syrian defence minister, arrived at the coffee-shop. Tlass is famous for his interest in flowers—he has published two books on the subject, and has dedicated a rose to President Assad. He is even more famous for his poetry, some of which is dedicated to Gina Lollobrigida. Other poems were written for a former 'Miss Lebanon'. In one poem he writes of rockets turning into roses. Tlass turned up at the coffee-shop in swimming trunks.

Tlass had heard that I had just finished writing a book about Lebanon. 'I hope you have written about our great victories against the Israelis in Lebanon. In 1982, I had 300 captured Israeli pilots but the Israelis claimed they had lost no aircraft—so where did the pilots come from?' There were roars of laughter around the table. The general smoothed his moustache, beamed at the women.

West Beirut, Tuesday 4 July

No sleep last night, very difficult to write today. Shells began hitting the neighbouring streets at nine o'clock this morning. Three window-shoppers were killed. I went out into the street and found people conducting normal business; they walked a little faster. But they were, unconsciously perhaps, showing their contempt for this 'war of liberation', 'war against Zionism', 'war against the "isolationists"' (the last a Syrian epithet for Aoun's supporters).

Saturday 22 July

My holiday is beginning. I drove up to Jounieh to take the hydrofoil to Cyprus. From there to Paris. The boat was to leave at midnight but my driver, who was a waiter at the Aquarium Hotel, insisted on getting me to the port before ten o'clock. 'After ten they go boom-boom,' he explained.

We reached the quay and Syrian shelling began. The Phalange militia had placed an artillery battery in the port and the Syrians in west Beirut were picking up its trajectory on their radar and firing back. The next few hours were grim. Shells were exploding around us and there was no sign of the boat. The hydrofoil arrived at two in the morning. The Phalange militiamen on the quay chose to inspect passports. Then, amid the shellfire, they counted the number of passengers. There were 300 or so. They counted again to confirm the first total. They stopped counting when shells started bursting in the water around them. We ran up the gangplank to the boat, the air hissing and cracking with the exploding shells.

Here was the war the journalists write about. It was now true to say that 'Syrian and Christian gunners pounded both sides of Beirut with their howitzers and Soviet-made Grad multi-barrelled rocket-launchers.' Howitzers, Grads by the dozen, heavy artillery, light artillery, shell-bursts at fifty to the minute. I watched the explosions diminish into pinpricks through the rear window of the hydrofoil as we moved out of Lebanese waters. In two weeks I would be back in Lebanon.

NOTES FROM ABROAD

Bogotá, Colombia
Roger Garfitt

Driving along la Séptima, the main road into the centre of Bogotá, we find ourselves blocked by a high-speed convoy. Two Toyota Land Cruisers are shepherding a black Mercedes. One hugs its back bumper. The other sways beside it in the outside lane. Then we glimpse the roof of a third in front. The back door of the rear Toyota is wavering, as if it's about to fly open. I can see a hand gripping the window-frame and I am expecting it to open the door and slam it properly shut. Until the door swings out on a bend and I see the neat black muzzle of a sub-machine-gun. The hand pulls the door to, as a woman might slip a bra strap back under her dress, but holds it ajar, ready to fling it open the moment the Mercedes is blocked. I think of one of the children's drawings *Semana* printed yesterday in an article on the psychological effects of the violence. Underneath the child had written: 'We're really afraid of the bodyguards. They're so edgy and they leap out of their cars and fire without thinking of the school buses going past with children in.'

Eugenia, meanwhile, is curious to see who's in the black Mercedes. She accelerates past the rear Toyota. This seems to me a little unwise but we're running into traffic now and the convoy itself accelerates, dodging left and right, wherever there's a gap, and swerving back into formation. The rear-gunner is ahead of us again, the back door veering open and the little black snake's tongue of the gun barrel flickering in and out. But no one's niftier than Eugenia in the hurtle and lurch of Bogotá traffic. As the convoy bears off to the right, she slips up on the inside. Someone we don't recognize, a man in his sixties with a bald spot in thick brown hair, is leaning back on the cushions and talking to an elegant grey-haired woman beside him. With his right hand he is making a slow gesture, as if, in the course of a reflective Sunday afternoon drive, he were developing some subtle point.

*T*here are no sodium lights in Bogotá. Street lighting is subdued and darkness presses down from the mountains, so thick you can almost rub it between your fingers.

Driving at night is like navigating between islands. You cross deep pools of tree shadow. The sunken lake of a park. Run across a strip of light—a shop-front, an office building—where the shadows are mobile. One leans out of a doorway. Another detaches itself from the angle of a wall. They are private security guards, a single-barrelled shotgun hung over their shoulder. Then trees and the long canal of the central reservation swallow you again. You pass a sentry-box at the entrance to a residential estate, a figure reading a newspaper in an oblong of light.

Every café and restaurant has its jetty, its strip of lit pavement. You pull in and an attendant comes to the edge. He motions you up to the kerb. He finds you a mooring. You almost expect him to throw you a rope.

These are the Fortunate Isles. Beyond lies the south of the city, an uncharted bayou where millions live in rudimentary houses, along unpaved roads.

Even those teeming alleys must be deserted now, the charcoal braziers of the roast corn-cob and kebab stalls smoking quietly into the night. Colombia's second city, Medellin, where the terrorists began, had thirty-seven bombs in a fortnight and was under curfew for three weeks. It took just one bomb to turn Bogotá into a ghost city after dark. That was the lorry bomb that cracked open the offices of *El Espectador* and covered the printing presses and the news desks in fallen plaster and broken glass. We live on the other side of the city but the rumble seemed to be right in our roof beams. At first, I thought the building's huge satellite dish, the size of a radio telescope, had collapsed.

Since then people have been taking no chances. By nine o'clock the streets are empty. Restaurants still open. Lamps burn on the quays. But the trees arch into the night, their dark masses unbroken. No flares of green from approaching headlights.

Last week a friend took us out to dinner. Entering the restaurant I felt like a coin clicking into the slot of a penny arcade. The waiters were standing between the empty tables with their arms folded. There was just one other couple, a pair of lovers at a corner table, locked into each other's gaze. Our penny dropped and the restaurant whirred into motion. The waiters crossed the floor. The barman clinked among his glasses. They took off the *boleros* and put on some *salsa*. But no one else dropped in and the machinery soon ran down. The waiters refolded their arms. The barman went back to his newspaper.

We sat by the window and looked down on to the still lights of the city. We were up on la Calera, the great ridge that rises to the north of Bogotá. A hundred feet of solid rock, I thought, between us and the road. Impossible to bomb.

The lovers were still there when we left. They had had a tiff, the man stiffening in his chair, the woman laughing and throwing her arms around his neck. Now she had him wound back into a close embrace. I saw their two cars, side by side in the car-park, and suddenly made the connection: it was the perfect time for an affair. They had the city to themselves.

*I*tend to gauge the level of tension by the number of soldiers in the next street. A Supreme Court judge lives there. Two years ago when I first came to Bogotá to join Eugenia for the summer, there were two soldiers outside day and night, guarding the building. Last year there were three. This year there are four.

They used to be very relaxed. I'd see one down at the phone box, ringing his girl-friend. Or borrowing the guitar from the man in the sweet stall and playing it with his sub-machine-gun slung across his back. Or I'd find one in front of me in the bakery. As we pressed towards the counter, the gun became like a shoulder-bag or an umbrella, one of those hard edges you mould yourself round in a queue. Its stubby snout nudged familiarly against my chest.

Now they are always along the kerb, checking on anyone who tries to park outside the building, or in front of the bank opposite. Car bombs are the latest weapon and suddenly everyone is vulnerable: the man in the black Mercedes because bodyguards are irrelevant and no one is quite sure whether a bullet-proof car can be made bomb-proof; and the rest of us because car bombs are indiscriminate. In May a car bomb on la Séptima just missed General Maza Márquez, the head of the Security Service, as a four-car convoy swept him to the office. Just missed because the terrorist was a fraction of a second late on the remote control and a passing Renault took the force of the blast. The General's bullet-proof car was wrecked and the convoy scattered across the road. But the real casualties were among the passers-by: a woman on the bus to work; a policeman walking home off the night shift; a little girl standing on the kerb, waiting for a school bus; and the man in the Renault, who just happened to be the father of an ex-Minister.

Every time we drive home, the one-way system takes us past the small skyscraper where the judge has his flat. Iron gates are drawn across the forecourt. The porter's lodge has dark, bullet-proof windows. At night it looks even more sinister. The light from the lodge catches on the soldier's helmets, on the fluorescent No Parking sign they move out into the road. The first time we saw them, we stopped and reversed out of the street.

By day, Bogotá's street life washes back in, the sellers of anything and everything, *salsa* on their portable radios, their street cries amplified through little hand-held loudspeakers, *¡Lavadoras! ¡Aspiradoras!* Washing Machines Repaired! Vacuum Cleaners!, a constant, irrepressible commerce. Twenty yards from their high-security zone, the solders have allowed two lads to set up a car-washing service. In this select street, tacked on to a telegraph pole, has appeared a split end of wood, a bit of broken plank or an old fencing slat, announcing in uneven white paint: wE wAsh aNd sHinE yOur caR. Trade doesn't seem to be brisk but the lads have brought a radio and lie on the grass, flipping through tabloids. Someone has set up another sweet stall. Bank messengers in their smart suits stop, and buy gum, and gossip.

At times street life makes security impossible. Every red traffic-light announces a two-minute market. Vendors move between the lines of cars, selling newspapers, duty-free Marlboro's, the latest García Márquez. Others offer home-made biscuits and sweets: light, crisp *obleas*, like huge communion wafers filled with *arequipe*, a kind of condensed milk; rounds of real gelatine, boiled from cows' bones and sweetened with cane sugar. Black women from Choco carry trays of *alegrías* on their heads, balls of popcorn stuck together with cane sugar. Children sell the fruits of Colombia's twice-yearly summers: little leathery-skinned tropical plums that explode on your tongue in a starburst of sweetness; *pomarrosas* that would have delighted Oscar Wilde because biting into them is like biting into a wad of rose petals. And sometimes, as happened last week in Medellin, threading through all this come gunmen posing as cigarette sellers, who shoot a former mayor as he sits between his chauffeur and his bodyguard, waiting at the lights.

*W*hat is at stake is the character of a country which, for all its problems, has always been a pleasure to live in. The drug barons are exerting their subtlest, most persuasive pressure on just this point. Life will not be worth living, they are saying, if the government does not negotiate. The recent bombs have not been intended to cause casualties, which would further unite the country against them. Placed in banks, building societies, schools and supermarkets at night, when the buildings are empty, they are designed to cause panic, to make people ask themselves, 'Where will it all end?'

Ironically, the more security measures the authorities impose, the more persuasive the blackmail becomes.

Threats can be almost as disruptive as bombs themselves. Calls have been made to schools and colleges, *el terrorismo telefónico*. Terrorists stole a van from the water company and toured Bogotá, broadcasting warnings that the supply had been contaminated. Poisoning on such a scale is actually almost impossible. Whole fleets of tankers would have to pump chemicals into the reservoirs, an operation that could hardly go unnoticed. But many people shut their water off. The authorities had to restore confidence by announcing that scientists were keeping a twenty-four-hour watch, testing the supply every hour.

Another rumour was that *el Día del Amor y la Amistad*, a kind of extended Valentine's Day in which families, lovers and friends all exchange presents, would turn into *el Día de la Muerte*. They would assassinate Barco. They would blow up the Presidential Palace. There were many variants.

El Día is one of the fiestas where families gather and drink rum and *aguardiente* and dance through till dawn. South Americans do not leap about, thumping the ground with their feet, as Europeans and North Americans do. They dance from the ground upwards. Their feet softly paddle and their hips begin to sway. It's the release of a communal rhythm. Children wriggle like elvers in a spring tide. The old yield to it gravely, like trees to the wind. And the young dance as angels might make love, their hips close, fluent and inexhaustible, their feet hardly touching the ground.

This year it was a sad day. The authorities pulled out all the stops. They mobilized the cadets from the army and police colleges. They blocked all the roads into Bogotá and searched everyone entering the city. The police chief appeared on television, exhorting people to go out and enjoy themselves. But the discothèques on la Calera stayed empty. The dance-floors in the small towns were closed.

T he drug barons are not the only ones contesting the ownership of Colombia. There are their old partners in the drug trade, the guerrillas. There are the right-wing death squads, originally financed by the drugs barons to settle accounts with the guerrillas when they fell out. And there are freelance criminals who disguise themselves as one or the other and learn from both.

The government has tried to open up the democratic process. It sponsored the formation of a new left-wing party, the *Unión Patriótica*, to give the guerrillas a political voice, only to find that 800 of its members—senators, congressmen, local mayors and councillors—have been assassinated in the last four years. And the killings do not stop there. The MOIR, a Maoist party that runs half of Colombia's trade unions, has had to withdraw its workers from some areas because they were being killed by the guerrillas. Liberal and Conservative politicians in the remoter regions are killed by whoever thinks they're in the way. And now there has arisen a new right-wing party, MORENA, the Movement for National Recovery, that has made some people fear Colombia could go the way of El Salvador.

It is not that Colombians are violent in themselves. Like the Irish, another nation with a violent history, they are a gentle, courteous people. But their geography is fierce. In Colombia the Andes split into three mountain chains. There are volcanoes, avalanches and landslides, like the one that buried Armero four years ago. There are rivers that flood twice a year. There is rain forest. There is desert. There are areas where communications are so difficult that the writ of central government hardly runs. Others where local corruption prevents it from running to much effect. Last year the governor of Nariño resigned after three days, declaring the department ungovernable.

In two areas, Pacho and Magdalena Medio, the drug barons had virtually created states within a state. Pacho is in the mountains of Cundinamarca, not far from Bogotá. It had been a poor town, fought over by the guerrillas. But it happens to be the home town of Rodriguez Gacha, one of the Medellin Cartel. When he made his millions from cocaine, he bought the town up and turned it into a baronial fief. Every outlying farm was equipped with a two-way radio to warn of the approach of guerrillas. Each district was patrolled by flying squads of heavily armed men in Jeeps. Luxury restaurants opened in the town centre. Gacha paid well and the whole area became a kind of high-life park. Now the army has occupied Pacho and the government has to provide for the people, replacing their artificial prosperity with some sustainable income.

Magdalena Medio is a more complex case. The best cattle country in Colombia, it was occupied by the guerrillas, who demanded a tithe from the poor and protection money from the rich. Some landowners sold up and drug barons bought their land cheaply. When the army moved back in, the landowners and peasants united against the guerrillas and formed self-defence groups. They were trained by Israeli instructors who entered Colombia legally. But the drug barons brought in other instructors, British and Australian mercenaries, who entered illegally and may well have created paramilitary units of a quite different kind. Somewhere out of that welter of armament and instruction came the massacres that shocked Colombia last year. Whole villages were wiped out, and then an entire judicial team that was investigating the massacres. The self-defence groups were banned, the land-owners and peasants protested, and out of that protest grew MORENA.

It does not take much political analysis to see that the drug barons are incidental to Colombia's real problems. They have simply acted as catalysts, precipitating an already unstable situation. Colombia is not a poor country. Always rich in agriculture, it now has coal and oil as well. But past mismanagement made it seem poor and created the conditions for the guerrillas, who are now seriously weakening the economy, even attacking the oil pipelines. The question is whether the government can achieve rapid enough social change by democratic means or whether the guerrillas will impose their own solution.

The government did succeed in San José de Guaviare, a cocaine-growing area that the army recaptured two years ago. Little more than a landing-strip in the jungle, San José had all the hallmarks of a town riding high on the drug boom. The shops along its one street stocked the mafia's favourite whiskies, Chivas Regal and Johnny Walker Black Label, while a single plantain, the food of the poor, cost two hundred pesos, five times the normal price. Legend had it that the army would never dare enter San José. But when helicopters came over the trees and launches came up the river, the guerrillas simply melted into the jungle. The army brought in more than troops: they brought in advisors. They suggested substitute crops, gave loans to buy seed, arranged transport to get the produce to market. They provided what had been missing for so long: development.

It's hard to imagine what under-development means until you have experienced it. Last year we had to queue on the road from Medellin to Barranquilla because a landslide had swept part of it away. The road, the only link between Colombia's main industrial city and its principal port, had been closed all weekend. Now it was open again, but only just. We sat in the Jeep, dwarfed by the huge *tractomulas* that haul Colombia's freight. Macks and Chevrolet Super Brigadiers, their cabs festooned with lights, their long bonnets carrying silhouettes of naked women on the radiator and a statue of the Virgin Mary on the air-filter. Three hours it took, inching forward through the rain, before we came to what they had managed to rebuild of the road: a single lorry's width of gravel and mud, shelving precariously on a steep hillside.

The usual vendors had appeared out of nowhere. They trudged along the line of lorries, offering peanuts roasted in cane sugar, bottles of *aguardiente*, cans of beer. One man had a big cardboard box of *saltinas*, salt biscuits. As he walked past us, the soggy cardboard finally gave way and the packets of biscuits spilled out on to the verge. He was gathering them up, trying to hold the box together with plastic and string, when he saw us watching him. He looked up and gave a wry smile: '*Vivir pobre es muy sabroso, gracias a Dios.*' 'Thank God, the life of the poor has a flavour all of its own.'

Notes on Contributors

Jonathan Raban's books include *Soft City, Coasting* and *Arabia Through the Looking Glass*. He recently wrote a pamphlet published in Chatto & Windus's 'Counterblasts' series entitled *God, Man and Mrs Thatcher*. **Rian Malan** was born into a prominent Afrikaner family in Johannesburg. He now lives in Los Angeles. His book, *My Traitor's Heart*, will be published early in 1990 by The Bodley Head and Atlantic Monthly Press. **Patrick Zachmann**'s Kowloon photographs are part of a project he is working on about the Chinese diaspora. **Tim O'Brien**'s novel, *Going After Cacciato*, which drew on his experience in Vietnam, received the National Book Award in the US. 'Quantum Jumps', his previous contribution to *Granta*, appeared in *Granta* 16, 'Science'. **Patrick McGrath** lives in New York. His first novel, *The Grotesque*, was published earlier this year, following a collection of his short fiction, *Blood and Water and Other Tales*. **Paul Theroux** is currently in New Guinea. His first travel book, *The Great Railway Bazaar* was published in 1975. **Patricia Highsmith** was born in Fort Worth, Texas and now lives in Switzerland. Her books include *Ripley's Game, Talented Mr Ripley* and *Strangers on a Train*. Penguin bring out a collection of her short stories in February. **Jill Hartley** is an American photographer living in Paris. An exile from Czechoslovakia after the events of 1968, **Josef Škvorecký** now lives in Toronto. His novels include *The Swell Season, The Engineer of Human Souls* and, most recently, *Dvorak in Love: A Light Hearted Dream*. **Robert Fisk** is Middle East correspondent for the *Independent* and lives in west Beirut. *Pity the Nation*, his book on Lebanon, will be published next year. The poet **Roger Garfitt** has spent his last three summers in Bogotá. His most recent volume of poetry is *Given Ground*. 'Summers in Norfolk' his previous contribution to *Granta* appeared in *Granta* 27, 'Death'.

NOTE: A *Granta* index covering issues 1 to 28, 1979 to 1989, is available for £4.99 from Granta, 44a Hobson Street, Cambridge CB1 1NL.